HOW TO BE A
PARANORMAL
DETECTIVE

GREG LAWSON
FOREWORD BY JEFF BELANGER

Visionary Living Publishing/Visionary Living, Inc.
New Milford, Connecticut

Front cover design by April Slaughter
Back cover and interior design by John Cheek

ISBN: 978-1-942157-48-9 (pbk)
ISBN: 978-1-942157-49-6 (epub)

Published by Visionary Living Publishing/Visionary Living, Inc.
New Milford, Connecticut
www.visionarylivingpublishing.com

For Craig Hutchinson,
my friend; an actual giant.

Acknowledgments

I would like to thank Amanda Heye-Landaker and Jennifer Readman for all the hard work and for sharing their insight of the paranormal with me. Thanks to Joy Pottinger-Baun for your keen eye and attention to detail. And to my wife, Lynn, for making my life fun.

Contents

Foreword

Jeff Belanger

So. you want to investigate the paranormal, huh? If you watch some of the many television shows on the subject, you might be making your checklist of things you'll need to get started:

EMF Meter... check
Audio recorder... check
Night-vision camera... check
Cool black t-shirt... check
Awesome acronym team name like:
Paranormal Observers Organization, or P.O.O. ... check

You're ready now, right? Not really. The gear is great, it's interesting—and some of it lights up and makes noise—but each item offers you only a tiny data point. There's no such thing as a "ghost detector."

If you want to simply look the part and storm out there in search of the unexplained tonight, then go ahead, put this book down now, and save your money.

But... if you want to learn something about investigating, and you want to get better at doing it yourself, and maybe make some serious contributions to a field of study that desperately needs better data and investigators... read on.

I first met Greg Lawson back in 2011 at the Central Texas Paranormal Conference. When I met him, he was in his sheriff's uniform. I played "Breaking the Law" by Judas Priest over the house speakers, and when Greg pulled out his police flashlight and flashed it on and off in time with the music, my first thought was: This guy can hang! I figured Lawson was there as some kind of security detail, but no, it turned out he also has a passion for the unexplained. We started talking and quickly became friends.

At a different event where both of us were speaking at the conference, we were leading a ghost hunt in a section with a psychic medium who was giving a kind of gallery reading to each group as they came in. Greg and I hung back while sharing skeptical glances at each other as we listened. After the reading, we led the group through the rest of the hour. The next group came in and the psychic started his second reading of the night, with Greg and me still in the back of the room. As the psychic repeated the same reading for the new group, Greg and I cocked our heads at each other... we smelled a rat.

We share a similar view that something weird is going on in the world, but there's an awful lot of noise out there. To cut through the noise, it takes dedication and a methodology. Who better to learn from about investigating than an actual police detective? Greg Lawson is a military veteran who has worked in law enforcement since 1986. He knows a thing or two about examining a crime scene, building a case, and presenting evidence before a judge and jury, because he's had to go through this process at major crime scenes, such as murders, where people's lives are on the line.

Given there aren't always security cameras around to catch criminals in the act, Greg understands he needs to build a case that proves a suspect perpetrated the crime beyond a reasonable doubt.

Let me repeat that: beyond a reasonable doubt.

Everything that bumps in the night isn't a ghost. Every witness didn't actually see a demon lurking in the shadows. Every blinking light in the sky isn't a UFO. And every strange print in the woods isn't a Bigfoot.

That being said, there are strange events occurring all around us. Given very few people in academia or the scientific community are looking into the unexplained, such investigation is left to devoted hobbyists around the globe. If we can up our game with proven techniques and methods, we will be taken more seriously by everyone, and maybe shed some light into what's actually going on.

Greg Lawson is the guy to help. In these pages, Greg offers a career's worth of knowledge and investigative experience, like how to interview witnesses, not compromise a crime scene, remain objective, and present your findings. Though we may not be trying to solve recent murders, these skills translate when it comes to investigating the unexplained. We can all learn something from Greg's vast know-how, and fortunately he presents it with some personality.

The truth is out there. *How to Be a Paranormal Detective* will help you find it.

Jeff Belanger is author of *The World's Most Haunted Places*, host of *30 Odd Minutes,* and writer/researcher for the *Ghost Adventures* show on the Travel Channel.

Preface

In 1980, the only thing I knew about paranormal investigation was what I learned from *The Amityville Horror* and *The Exorcist*. There may have been some other movies I had seen from that time in my life, but they made no real impact in my view of the unexplained.

You must remember, there were only three network television channels and independent movie theaters at the time (HBO was in its infancy opening what ultimately became a larger distribution of programing), so exposure to the paranormal was limited. To say I knew nothing of paranormal investigations at that time would be truly accurate. Of the loosely defined ghost hunting groups I was involved with in high school, they were ad hoc teams of teenagers equipped with fast cars, intoxicants, and uninvolved parents. While Austin, Texas remains my home of record, I was formed to be who I am in a small town known as Rockdale. Rockdale is like many other small towns in Texas, a slave to a couple of large industries, fanatic in sports, mainly football, and subject to boredom. But I think being bored is a condition of genetics and upbringing, because I and a select few other friends were never bored. If we were not out exploring the woods, finding somewhere to swim, chasing girls, or tying kites to the top of microwave relay towers, we were sneaking out at night, driving fast, smoking cigarettes, swimming in water towers, and trying to buy beer. Somewhere in between this entertainment and school we explored the haunted legends and lore of our county: Crybaby Bridge, the Blackjack Monster, The Colonel,

Pleasant Hill Cemetery, and Tanglewood Forest. All of these were unique to themselves, until I travelled away from my patterned geography and realized just about every town has a Crybaby Bridge, a large monster cat, and a local cemetery that feeds the imagination of kids and facilitates reasons to take girlfriends to remote and scary places.

While I enjoyed *Ghostbusters* and a few other pseudo-paranormal movies, it wasn't until the TV series *Ghost Hunters* was broadcast on mainstream TV that I became aware of the broad work being done in the area of the supernatural. Later, researchers and archivists such as Rosemary Ellen Guiley, Fiona Broom, John Zaffis, Linda Moulton Howe, Don Schmitt, Tom Carey, and Richard Dolan really spurred my interest in the methodology and techniques of investigating the paranormal. While collegiate work is conducted to explain certain observable phenomena, much of the real experimentation and research is done at the grass roots level by dedicated hobbyists. Many of these groups around the nation and around the world have brought some of the most intriguing examples of paranormal experience to light. Some of these have provided invaluable observations and explanations of such experiences and have refined the idea of paranormal possibilities. With this book, my intentions are to outline investigative skills in a contemplative way. Investigations are not static; they are fluid and require conceptual thought, and not a step one, two, three approach. While I have travelled extensively with the US military throughout America and Europe with my wife, Lynn, my exposure dedicated to the paranormal is limited by time spent on site. Although I have toured some of the most haunted places on the planet, I have had inadequate investigative time at most. I began to think, what would be the best way I could be a part of the paranormal investigative society and have the most impact? Using my limited time investigating a few sites in the southwest, or writing an investigative book and helping the truly dedicated researchers throughout the world conduct chronological and concise explorations of their chosen phenomena?

My hopes are, that with the information in this book, devoted paranormal investigators can increase their understanding of human interaction with the paranormal and bring us closer to the answers to the questions we are asking. It is to these people that I salute; the ones who won't quit under pressure or back down under scorn until our questions are answered.

The ones who strive to be paranormal detectives.

Introduction

Man has searched for the afterlife since before recorded time. On every continent and throughout every culture man has possessed the desire to understand his world and the cosmos—life and the afterlife. Runes etched into rock or ink pressed to paper, the evidence of man's search is all around us. We need to know, we desire to know, we must know. It's what we do. There are many beliefs and many ways to practice those beliefs, but one thing remains the same: man strives for not only knowledge but also experience. He has gone so far as to starve himself, induce dangerous drugs or substances derived from plants and animal venoms, and endured ritualistic pain, including self-flagellation, in order to attain a spiritual experience, a mystical understanding, or a divine state of consciousness. These experiences are often referred to as transpersonal—the struggle to achieve a conscious experience beyond human limits. It is in this inherent human pursuit which we strive for increased self-development, peak experiences of pure joy or elation and the potential of metaphysical capabilities.

In contrast to our search for meaning, there are distractions that complicate this pursuit. Event experiences can be as different as euphoria is to terror and everything in between. When these happenings are examined properly, we must consider that each are often related to the experiencer in a contemporary context. One can see the evolution of these experiences in the reporting of phenomena of the day. As technology changes, so does the human experience. Today's dream paralysis was once referred to as an Old Hag experience in Old English lore. It is described as the feeling that the dreamer has someone, such as an old hag or demon, sitting on the dreamer's chest and not allowing them to breath or move. In my experience, these occurrences are now more often reported in the ufology community when referring to abduction experiencers. The event is indicated by intense fears, inability to move or breathe, and the feeling that something evil is near. In some cases, the experiencer reports seeing these entities.

To an extent, through our training and experience, we shape our own perception. Typically, we only know, what we know. Every day we walk among the living we are exposed to new experiences, people, and things. It is our individual perception that molds our day; our interpretation of these experiences, people, and things provide an intellectual and emotional outcome. Our base values, assumptions, beliefs, and expectations (VABEs) forge our perceived world. The VABEs are four sets of "rules" that form what a person inherently expects from the actions and people in their surroundings. I am often disappointed in these expectations. For many years, I was so surprised that people didn't think the same way I did. That they did not value the life of a person or the treatment of an animal the way I did. I assumed that people try to make the right decision and believe that the Catholic Church is the direct route to God, and I always expected that I would be treated fairly. My VABEs have backfired on me a time or two. Now, when dealing with another person, I try to take their VABEs into consideration before I even attempt to understand their position.

The perception of the paranormal experience is all about interpreting the stimulus (the paranormal activity) using your own values, assumptions, beliefs, and expectations. Rosemary Ellen Guiley speaks extensively throughout the country on interpretations of experience. Through her extensive understanding of the paranormal, she believes many of the occurrences today and throughout history have been Djinn beings misidentified as spirits, extraterrestrials, shadow figures, aliens, demi-gods, and human creature hybrids. Through paranormal interdisciplinary study, Guiley has isolated behavior that, when classified, points toward her assertion of the Djinn culprit and their malicious activities toward man.

These interpretations of paranormal events can vary widely given the disciplinary approach to the investigation and the investigator's education, training, and experience. It is the investigator's approach that will expose the truth or distract from it. While the proper use of anomaly detection equipment is paramount, the investigators' ability to separate themselves from their man-made tools and take in the experience may be the real investigative skill.

Is it possible that the paranormal experience is solely observed by the human condition? Could experience possibly originate from another dimension, another plane, another time or space that can be detected only by your mind, spirit, or instinct? Could it be that the manifestation is occurring right in front of you while you are instead staring intently at your electronic spirit box? Nearest I can tell, many of these tools have not proven the existence of any spirit, and hauntings have abounded far before the invention of electricity. I believe we may have been born with our detectors: natural human intuition, instinct, insight, or unexplainable sensitivities. Some are just better than others.

Sometimes people approach a situation in the exact opposite way I would, yet they accomplish the same goals I would have set for the outcome. Recently, I watched a documentary involving an "animal communicator" and an abused, black leopard. The cat had been transferred from a situation of abuse to a rescue habitat. The cat refused interaction and would not come out of its cage to explore its surroundings for over six months. The caretakers tried everything, and one worker was severely injured by the animal. As a last-ditch effort, they brought in a type of medium referred to as an animal communicator. This person sat with the cat and reported to have communicated with it. They said the cat told them it did not like its name, was concerned about some other cats that were left behind at the zoo where he was found and did not like humans. The animal communicator said they put the cat at ease by telling it they would change his name, that the two young cubs back at the zoo where he had been were fine and explained that the handler respected the cat. After six months in its cage, the cat came out and socialized the same day the animal communicator spent time with him.

I do not pretend to understand what happened in this case. Conventional wisdom would tell me telepathy with an animal is impossible. Even if it was possible, how could the cat speak English, or the communicator speak feline? Or, maybe it's something else? Regardless of my confusion on the matter, after the animal communicator's interaction with the cat, the cat's behavior changed. The constant growling stopped, and he began to interact with his surroundings in an inquisitive and encouraging way. No matter the method, the outcome of the interaction with the animal communicator was a positive one.

Throughout this book, I give many case examples with some of them identified as fraud. These examples are by no means the norm—they are merely facts you should consider, and they come in many forms. Even if you are doubtful of a belief, theory, or method, if the intent is positive, what is the harm in trying to understand or trying to make things better? As a paranormal investigator, do not discount any possibilities. Remain open-minded but wary of misinterpretation. The intent of this book is to assist you in these endeavors.

PART ONE
The Investigative Process

CHAPTER 1

Why We Are Here

There is a reason you are reading this book. There may be many—curiosity, research, or fun. Whatever the reason, the ideas and methods conveyed in these pages can be applied to many situations in life, not just paranormal investigations.

What's It All About?

Many people in the paranormal field find a connection to others in the field. Sharing similar questions and perceptions of the world with others who are less likely to judge makes for safe exploration. We are all about the possibilities and searching for answers that many of the masses never contemplate. People existing day-to-day, getting up, going to work, paying bills, rinsing and repeating, often never allow themselves to dwell intensely on the question: "What is this all about?" That is what investigation addresses. And that's what we are going to do in the following pages. We are going to identify what a paranormal investigation is and how we go about conducting it to avoid negligence and irresponsibility. We want to circumvent the realm and stigma of cases like the Austin Yogurt Shop Murders, as you will see in the next chapter. A who-done-it murder is hard enough to solve, a who-done-it covered by arson is a huge endeavor. And an arson-murder who-done-it without employing industry standard methods and techniques will result in a train wreck. And as you will see, it did.

What's Behind the Curtain?

In 1970, when I was a child, I was so shocked that some dude was faking being the Wizard of Oz; what a huge let down that was! After watching that movie, I began to look more critically at everything. I remember in first grade we had to put together a map of the world using simple puzzle pieces of the continents. I took the pieces and stuck them all together into one landmass. I was amazed at how closely they seemed to fit together; not perfect, but close. My teacher, Mrs. Cloud, came over and corrected me. She showed me how to put the pieces in their proper place. Then she pulled them back out and shuffled the seven pieces and told me to try it again. I told her that I thought they all fit together at one time and they simply floated apart. Mrs. Cloud corrected me and said, "No, they have always been like they are now." I do not feel that I had some sort of previous life insight to the shape of the original Earth island of Pangaea; the pieces just seemed to fit. And it is typical of an uninquisitive person to just color inside the lines or fit each piece into the expected space.

I have found that each paranormal investigation is like my 1970s world puzzle map; you can see where the pieces fit and be done with it, or you can be creative and look further, behind that curtain. Even though each paranormal investigation is unique, certain things keep reoccurring. Orbs, shadows, strange noises and feelings are all part of solving the mystery and deciding where they fit. Many times, people have experiences that automatically fit into their paradigm, and to them, the mystery is solved. But I say, let's look behind the curtain.

EXAMPLE: Pleasant Hill Cemetery—near Rockdale, Texas

On October 31, 1980, I, along with Mike Crawly, Joe Cox, and Robert Pounders packed up Joe's 1972 Cutlass station wagon with camping gear, Micky's Malt Liquor, Sloe Gin, Marlboro cigarettes, and snacks, and headed for Pleasant Hill Cemetery for Halloween night. Pleasant Hill was a small community cemetery, church, and schoolhouse built around 1910. The grounds were maintained by a trust or organization and the church and schoolhouse, while old, were in good repair, even though they had been abandoned for years. The church was standard pier and beam construction, wooden pews, and altar with an old dilapidated piano. The school was small and had two classrooms separated by what looked to be a kitchen with a pot-bellied stove. The two buildings sat on either side of the cemetery with the old dirt road leading to the cemetery gate.

The one seriously unique thing about Pleasant Hill cemetery is that it was positioned in the middle of the coal strip mines that fed the electric generators for a large power plant and was the energy source for the locals and for Alcoa's aluminum smelting operation. The strip mines surrounded the cemetery on three sides and provided an unnatural valley for the graves. During the day, it was simply a well-manicured cemetery with a clean, whitewashed church and schoolhouse with boarded-up windows; at night it became something different, altogether.

I think it was Mike Crawly (AKA: Creepy Crawly) who had the idea to go to Pleasant Hill and camp out on the altar for Halloween, but all four of us agreed it was a great idea. We had all heard the stories about Pleasant Hill, the noises, the sound of footsteps in the schoolhouse, the flaming tombstones. We either wanted answers or the experience—I am not sure which.

Once we got to the church, we jimmied the side door and unloaded our battlewagon. Within minutes, the car was hidden behind the schoolhouse and we were in for the night. It was the beginning of ghost stories, tales about girls, and Robert's ghost storybook readings, all bathed in the light of flickering candles. By midnight Crawly was passed out cradling a bottle of Mickey's. Then, it was Robert face down and snoring. Joe, while chain-smoking his Marlboros, picked up Robert's book and quietly read out loud. Within minutes, I experienced what I perceived as my first paranormal encounter.

I was 16 years old.

For me, this was it. Up to that point, I had been searching for this my entire life. Not constant, not every day, but the questions were always there. The questions remain: Is there more? What is this all about? Why am I here? Being a confirmed Catholic at the time, and now, a recovering Catholic, I know the tales of the Bible, of spirits, of angels, of demons, and of death and the resurrection. I learned of regret and guilt. Penitence and suffering.

In fourth grade, I remember turning off my bedroom light and challenging Satan to appear. I remember seeking out the scary things and demanding proof. I remember cursing the darkness and laying in silence. Then sleeping soundly.

I don't do that so much anymore. Any of it.

When the sound started, it seemed nothing more than a fingernail scape on the wall of the church. Joe stopped reading and we looked at each other, both asking in our own minds, "Did you hear that?" Our eyes told each other we had. Joe started to say something, and it happened again, but this time there was a moan from the entire building; the whole church seemed to move, its old wooden skeleton grinding against itself.

I looked over and Robert lay silent. I kicked Crawly to wake him up, but he lay there and just continued to breathe.

I didn't.

The church moved again with the low moan and scraping sound. Dust long settled between the ceiling boards sprinkled down and dispersed in the stale air. Again the building shifted; this time all the lines in the interior of the church seemed to alter with a loud bang, as if a huge force had hit the wall. Then the church moaned again, as if waking from a long, troublesome sleep. I rose to my feet. Joe grabbed my calf and simply said, "No." But I had to see. Then, as now, I am an evidence guy; I need to see, connect the physical with the event. I carefully stepped to the side door of the church, grabbed the old doorknob, and slowly turned it. When the latch-bolt clicked and cleared the strike plate, I slowly pulled it open and worked my way around it, trying to get a glimpse of what was outside. Even though the candles provided some light, my eyes had not adjusted to the darkness. The strip-mine hills and woods beyond the spill of the candlelight were completely black and indistinguishable. Unfortunately, it was not a full moon, although it would not have mattered; an entire bank of low hanging clouds moved slowly across the sky and would have hidden it. Again the church moaned, and some wood creaked and cracked as I witnessed the door frame I was standing in bow at least an inch and the entire wall lean slightly, as if pushed by some great beast. Joe was on his feet now and had kicked Crawly a second time. I leaned farther to get my head out and around the frame. Farther, a little farther. Slowly, taking slices of a visual pie, one at a time I pushed forward and tried to retain my balance.

When I first saw it, I wasn't sure. Its mass was diffused in the darkness. Each time I moved forward a little, it grew larger and larger. It was dark; its outline was barely distinguishable with the blackness of its surroundings. The only contrast was the white schoolhouse in the background, which now appeared as a dark gray box. As my vision cleared the door jam, and I was able to employ both eyes, I froze, taking in the form of the thing's entire shape. The body. The legs. The head. My diluted brain dissected the shadows, shapes, and forms, shuffling and reassembling them into my idea of what would be trying to attack four teenagers in a church on Halloween night. Trying to make sense of what massive evil creature would use such brute force to topple down this sacred building onto four innocent kids of Rockdale. As the church creaked again, and as the dust drifted down from the cracks in the ceiling and around the doorframe, my brain arrived at a moment of clarity. And I knew what it was that I saw.

It was one of the largest cows I had ever seen, scratching its butt on the side of the church.

Welcome to paranormal research. But imagine what story would we have told if I had just done what Joe said? If I had stayed put and hadn't looked behind the curtain?

CHAPTER 2

The Act of Knowing

There are only three ways a person knows about something: (1) they are told about it, (2) they witnessed it, or (3) they did it. That my friends, is how we know.

Seems simple enough, right? You get the story, view the scene, gather the evidence, and then solve the mystery. I wish that was all there was to it; many paranormal investigators treat knowing as such. They suppose the statements made are true, they believe the location is accurate, and deem the evidence to be genuine. They package it up and present it as fact. In my experience of over 25 years working in investigations, this scenario is rarely true. While these steps should never be overlooked, there is much more to it.

EXAMPLE: The Yogurt Shop Murders—Austin, Texas

It was Friday, December 6, 1991, minutes before midnight when an Austin Police patrol officer reported smoke coming from a strip center near Northcross Mall. Later that night, 17-year-old Eliza Thomas, 13-year-old Amy Ayers, and sisters, 17-year-old Jennifer and 15-year-old Sarah Harbison, were found stripped, bound, gagged, and shot in the burned remains of the I Can't Believe It's Yogurt! shop at the corner of Anderson Lane and Rockwood Drive. Their bodies were found only after the fire was extinguished. Three lay stacked atop each other, charred to the bone. Ten years later, convictions were handed down from a Travis County jury for Robert Springsteen and Michael Scott. Both were subsequently overturned and the men were released. Charges on two other named accomplices, Maurice Pierce and Forrest Welborn, were dropped after two Travis County grand juries failed to indict them.

While the Austin Police handled the scene to the best of their limited ability, the Texas Department of Public Safety (DPS) crime lab processed the scene. A gap of about four hours later created the confusion that would haunt the case for the next decade. Four hours is not at all a long time to wait for firefighting officials to extinguish and deem an area safe for crime scene processing. However, the damage done by the extinguishing medium, in this case, water, and the number of persons entering the area and moving items and evidence, took their toll on the investigation. In court, it was discovered that Austin Police officials never fully contained the scene and never created a crime scene log to record who entered and exited the area—one of the very first things a responding officer should always implement. DPS investigator Irma Rios testified at trial that the on-scene investigation was not coordinated. She stated that no grid search was done and many things that were potential evidence were not collected. They even failed to process the shop's bathrooms, front door, and dumpster, a place known for criminals to dispose of evidence after a crime. These are industry standard practices for crime scene investigation; it's basic recruit academy 101. Ultimately, investigators did not collect a single piece of evidence that would connect any of the suspects to the murders.

Not one.

During the span of the investigation, more than 50 people have confessed to the murders, implicating themselves in a whole host of manners. Most of these confessors either did not know certain specifics of the scene or provided testimony contrary to the evidence and eliminated themselves from the possibility of being a suspect. As investigators, there is an art form to uncover the details and recreate an event to establish the holes in the story. It is vital to follow established protocol. Such details are critical for an investigator to be aware of. Specific scene details, known only to the suspect, began leaking out and eliminating the chances of narrowing in on a suspect.

Ten years later, although Robert Springsteen identified more details unknown by the other suspects, any usable evidence was lost through the lack of protocol. The Austin Yogurt Shop Murders remain officially, unsolved.

Investigation

Our ultimate paranormal research goal is to observe or study by close examination and systematic inquiry and to gather evidence of an event that is occurring or has occurred. This investigative process contains several basic steps that will lead the investigator to another series of steps. These steps are unique to the investigation. They can be interviewing victims, witnesses, and suspects. Surveying the scene. Identifying, photographing, and collecting evidence, and so on. New investigators often rely on a list they follow to ensure they cover everything and stay on track. Law enforcement investigations can range from the relatively simple crime with a witness and evidence, to an international crime with no leads. While each one will in a microcosm be conducted in much the same manner, one will undoubtedly require more steps.

To generalize a basic investigation, when law enforcement responds to a crime, they go to the scene, conduct interviews, establish corpus delicti (body of the crime), determine whether a crime was committed, document and collect evidence, assign blame, and write a concise report which may be referenced later by a detective. While the order of steps can vary, paranormal investigations are much the same. The major benefit being that paranormal investigations are rarely time sensitive. Paranormal investigators have the luxury of a larger span in which to gather information. Therefore, researching the location, people, and event prior to going to the site is efficient and adds to the excitement. This will allow the investigator to get a good first impression on the credibility of the person reporting, create a potential background story of the location, and determine what equipment would be best suited to the investigation.

In law enforcement, for an action to be a crime, it first must break a law. To judge this, a group of reasonable people get together and decide what the facts are to support the claim. It should be addressed that same way with a paranormal event. These elements should be identified in such a way as to build credibility, or the likelihood of such an event occurring within this time, at this place.

Paranormal events could be examined by the following fundamental elements:

Location. Does the site lend itself to the suggestion that a paranormal event would be likely to occur, i.e. the battlefield at Gettysburg, the pyramid at Giza, or the Lizzie Borden house?

Events. Are there multiple reports of paranormal events occurring at the site?

Explanation. Can the events be explained by conventional means, i.e. orbs caused by dust particles, electronic voice phenomena due to radio bleed-over, or electromagnetic readings due to hidden electric wall circuits?

Eventually, every investigation ends and is assigned a closure rating. It is that ending you, as a paranormal investigator, strive to get correct. It is your determination that fellow investigators and whoever else will scrutinize after reviewing your work. In doing so, you can claim one of three paranormal possibilities:

Founded. Physical evidence that leads a credible and reasonable person to believe a paranormal event occurred.

Unfounded. A natural occurrence was determined to be the cause of the event.

Undetermined. The lack of physical evidence or occurrence led to the impossibility of making a determination.

Undetermined is the unofficial primary closure for most paranormal investigations. However, essentially this is what we are deciding: (1) it is, (2) it is not, or (3) we don't know. Very few recorded events may be considered a "Founded" closure based on physical evidence and the totality of the circumstances. That is why it is so important that your investigation is methodical and well documented. While many shows rely on the abundant anomalous evidence observed at established locations, determining the actual phenomena is truly difficult. When I investigate, I do it for the excitement, for the intrigue—not for the closure code. However, if I were to find something legitimate and want to present it as fact, there needs to be a logically valid approach to the method. Educating yourself to make that determination is vital and attaining the ability to differentiate the normal from the paranormal is paramount.

Hunter vs. Investigator

To determine whether you are a hunter or investigator, ask yourself what kind of impact you want to have on people's lives, and what level of involvement matches your motivation. Are you *Star Trek* or *Star Wars*, *Lost* or *Gilligan's Island*, *Scooby-Doo* or *Ghostbusters*? Determine your mindset before you set sail. If you choose to be at times both a hunter and investigator, that is cool too, just recognize where and when to switch roles.

To some, there is no difference between the words hunter and investigator, but for purposes of evaluating your level of involvement, we will use the word investigator to indicate acts that are more thorough and researched. An investigator is someone who wants to present a complete report and provide recommendations when applicable. A hunters someone who takes a less formal approach, someone who is more interested in the adventure and reports findings as a topic of interest rather than as facts. Often, a hunter will assist more in an investigation event itself rather than research or evaluate the evidence of an investigation.

Distinguishing between the two is important, as in the example of ghost hunting. The amount of energy and seriousness devoted to an investigation might have a direct effect on a person's life. If you are invited into a home, provide a well-grounded haunting report, and as a result that homeowner moves because you are seen as the trusted expert, your actions carry weight. Consider your moral obligation in how you sell and present yourself, in the intensity behind the research, and in how your actions reflect on your fellow investigators.

There is also a motivational issue for you to identify and decide. Are you hunting to find out the what or are you investigating to find out the why? The fundamental mindset is the key to how a person approaches an investigation. Some cops try to get to the truth while others try to have the highest arrest rate in the unit. It's all about mind-set. Paranormal investigators should remain impartial and allow everyone to manage their roles/responsibilities and let the investigation provide the truth. In doing so, an investigator should not attempt to exhibit expertise in all fields of the paranormal nor discuss uncorroborated details with anyone outside their investigative circles until a definitive conclusion has been determined. By doing so, you could damage your credibility by revealing generalized conclusions. You can also taint the "jury pool," so to say. You don't want to groom other investigators by telling them what they can expect; in law enforcement interrogations, that is considered coaching the suspect or leading the witness into saying what you want. Many parents do this with their children in preparation for being interviewed. Coaching looks bad in court, and if you do it, it will reflect poorly on you as well.

Traits of an Investigator

In any research project, certain personality characteristics will be useful to the investigator: (1) unregulated suspicion, (2) morbid curiosity, (3) keen observance, and (4) skilled communication.

(1) Unregulated suspicion is what opens the investigation to all possibilities. Any investigator, whether doing background investigations for pre-employment new-hires or overseeing insurance fraud, should take nothing for granted. During an examination, the investigator may find that victims and witnesses may be motivated by various physiological, psychological, and sociological needs that may influence the information they give. These will need to be closely examined.

(2) Along with suspicion, morbid curiosity is a necessity for good, thorough work and will drive the investigation forward. An investigator must have the desire to investigate and learn the facts and truths about people, places, things and ideas. This means being habitually curious about

things such as spontaneous statements by witnesses that seem off topic or change the direction of the interview.

(3) Keen observations are why investigators are called trained observers. They should develop the ability to take accurate notice of, keep in view, and give attention to, those things that are monitored by our five (or maybe six) senses. In many cases, it can be the tiniest of observations that leads to a breakthrough in the case.

(4) Skilled communication, in many instances, will be the thing that gleans the most important information about the paranormal event and provides ideas on how to set up the best approach to observe it. Your ability to build rapport with the witness or experiencer will help free their memory and divulge every bit of relevant information they are likely to possess; skilled communication is the prime facilitator of the investigation. You gather good information through patience, professionalism, empathy, and above all else, skilled listening.

Whether a hobbyist or a professional, the investigator should have a certain skill set to be able to conduct an inquiry. In establishing a great skill set, the investigator should practice and work toward:

1. The ability to interview and passively interrogate witnesses.
2. The knowledge of how to research past events using records.
3. The skills to locate and assess the actual event location.
4. The ability to plan and organize a research event.
5. The experience of effectively choosing and using equipment.
6. The experience of effectively capturing the event on video.
7. The proficiency to prepare concise and chronological reports.
8. The professionalism to present the findings in an effective way.

Paranormal investigators should always strive to learn more about their chosen discipline and remain open to critique and learning from their and others' mistakes. Doing so will bring you one step closer to becoming a detective.

CHAPTER 3

Investigative Mindset

In law enforcement, there are technicians and there are theorists. Technicians typically work from a strict set of policies and procedures that moves their processes forward, step one, step two and step three. They have manuals and sets of lists in order to keep themselves on track, pace their progress, and record their actions. They are normally not interested in the concept of why, just that each of the processes are thoroughly conducted and recorded. On the other hand, theorists often skip, omit, or overlook items in a list that may not be related to the specific investigation. Often times, they may not use any type of form or list; instead, they follow an established investigative methodology that leads them to a solution. Both styles are proven to work; it is simply a matter of preference.

Technician or Theorist
Whether you are the technician or the theorist, the investigation itself is not about filling out a questionnaire or completing the tasks on a list. It is about recognizing different investigative processes, understanding human behavior, identifying inconsistencies, and utilizing those tools that work best for you. Using a list to ensure you don't miss anything is a good practice, but get your eyes off the paper, off your instrumentation, and pay attention to what is going on around you. Do not rely on your list. Instead, strive to understand the concepts of the investigative methods you choose. Whether your investigative method is (1) intuitive and based on mediumship, (2) a technical approach using strict rules and mechanical sensors, (3) observationally

based relying on human physical senses, or (4) logically based employing a scientific method, consistency is important. By being consistent, you and those who review your work will have an established baseline with which to gage the level of paranormal involvement and the proposed causes. However, limiting yourself to one particular method may minimize your findings; therefore, it is wise to have a wide understanding of many methods and know how they can work together and often complement each other.

Interdisciplinary Approach

An interdisciplinary approach goes hand-in-hand with any investigation. Paranormal investigators need to know not only about the paranormal but also about the various causes that may make something appear unusual when it is anything but. I will often run into someone who finds out that I am a detective and expresses that they too would like to be a detective. They ask about schools, certifications, and degrees. They say they have seen commercials advertising associate and bachelor degrees in police science and forensics. When I explain that in the agency where I work, home to one million people, there may be 30 crime scene specialists employed, they look at me in puzzlement. I explain that the way to become a detective is to become a cop or private investigator first. Both studies have a core set of skills but approach detective work in different ways. After fundamental training, you would gain experience and specialize from there. It would be impossible to conduct a law enforcement investigation within an organization with no education on required policies and procedures. And as every state and every jurisdiction is different, crime scene specialists are even more rare.

Most good detectives use an interdisciplinary approach to their investigations. Law enforcement detectives use (1) police sciences to guide their procedures, (2) sociology to interact with the community and conduct interviews, (3) criminology to research offenses and trends, (4) psychology to understand behavior and motivations, and (5) political science and law to navigate the investigative outcome. Tax and federal benefit fraud investigators do the same; they just might not fall under the same police sciences or political pressures. It's the same with child protective services or the railroad commission. Every investigation has its specialty. The paranormal field is no different. Closely studying paranormal phenomena in order to identify "them" or "it," for what "they" or "it" is reveals an interesting pattern; when we identify an unknown, we use our past experiences and understandings to form an impression. That impression is like a mental evidence locker. We fill our lockers with whatever related evidence we decide is proof, and this crafted opinion is safeguarded and resistant to change. An avid UFO hunter would be more likely to classify the shadow person as a cloaking, phase-shifting, or time-traveling extraterrestrial. It follows that the layman demonologist might consider an evil force before concluding it is an extraterrestrial. The Bigfoot hunter would prefer to associate those unknown screams, howls, and forest fall sounds to Sasquatch rather than a haunting. We relate to what we expect, and we can expect only what we understand.

Don't get me wrong; all of these disciplinary approaches, extraterrestrial, religious, cryptid, and spiritual, have documented and historical lore to support them. Each approach has its purpose. Specialization on a particular school of thought or subject is how humanity masters that subject. Math, chemistry, physics or biology are better understood when they are intensely studied. But when implementing these disciplines, understanding how each affects the other in order to create concepts or solve problems allows for a greater grasp of the bigger picture. To consider quantum mechanics is to meld both chemistry and physics into one study. That is why competent paranormal researchers adopt an interdisciplinary approach to their investigations. Cryptid hunters do well to have a broad familiarity in biology, ecology, and wildlife management. Ghost hunters should be knowledgeable about where to research the local history and lore, and they should be practiced in photography, videography, audiology and the proper use of environment monitoring equipment (not just EVPs). The UFO researcher should be familiar with aspects of astronomy and astrophysics and be conscious of airborne detection and tracking equipment, commercial flight corridors, satellite identification measures, and manmade things that are commonly misidentified as UFOs. Demonologists should have a working background of religious studies, human psychology, and, as with all disciplines, other possible misinterpreted paranormal phenomena or mistaken explainable events.

Most importantly, an investigator should have the ability to recognize the signs and symptoms of mental illness or chemical induced psychosis. But remember, just because a witness is having psychological disturbances, doesn't mean what they are telling you is not true.

Initial Concepts

The major difference between law enforcement and paranormal investigations is that law enforcement must follow the rule of law, the Constitution, the Amendments, federal law, state law, federal and state case law, departmental policies, city and county ordinances, and the rules set down verbally by your boss; paranormal investigations do not—generally. Paranormal investigations, while necessary to maintain the law, have very few established and sanctioned guidelines, procedures, and rules of evidence that prove legitimacy for your case. However, keep in mind that inconsistent methods, unprofessional behavior, and poor interpretations of the events can get the most arguable evidence flushed right down the toilet, along with your reputation.

It is imperative that you begin and end your investigation on a strong foundation. Focus on these concepts: (1) document the legend, (2) research the facts of the story, (3) identify any witnesses, (4) identify area experts and obtain statements from them, (5) recon the site for dangers to the crew, (6) identify detection equipment hazards, (7) coordinate the dates and times of the sightings, if possible, (8) secure the site, (9) conduct an operational briefing, (10) use a psychic resource if applicable, (11) set up video, audio, temperature, magnetic, radiation, and electronic monitoring, (12) monitor the readings without outside influence, (13) slowly input human interactions and communication, (14) recover equipment, (15) conduct a team leader debriefing, (16) conduct a team debriefing, (17) analyze the gathered data, and (18) make a determination.

Let's focus closer on each one of these topics:

Document the legend. This is one of the fun parts. Here you simply gather as much information from as many sources as possible and condense the information into one amalgamated account of the event. It is important to be selective in your accumulation of story information and cite your references. Even though it is a legend, be selective in your sources. Be aware that some tellers of tales will dramatically embellish their story if they stand a chance at being the one cited for bringing it to light.

Research the facts. Are there historical documents that support the legend? Every paranormal investigator or group should know how to access the historical society in their area. Historical societies typically have much of the newspaper and governmental documentation at their disposal. So many of the stories told in an area get changed over time. Sometimes the stories migrate with the people who tell them. Others hear them, get a little of the story wrong, then repeat it to someone else, and so on, and so on. Historical documents provided by the local library, newspaper office, county court house, U.S. Census Bureau, insurance companies, and other record keeping organizations can be extremely valuable in sorting out what the real event was and what it was not.

Identify witnesses. Witnesses are those who experience the event firsthand, who were told about the event by someone who actually experienced the event, or someone with knowledge of the event.

Identify area experts. Obtaining supportive information from experts is an important part of your research. Finding such persons to review your findings or to answer pertinent questions lends legitimacy to your process. Experts can be a local historian, librarian, or expert working in the field being investigated. Attempt to obtain official statements from them, written or digitally recorded.

Recon the site for dangers. Make sure you survey the site in daylight and identify any dangers to the crew. This also includes looking for additional evidence that may debunk an event.

Identify detection equipment hazards. Ensure you locate anything that could interfere with the detection equipment you are using. If you are using handheld CB radios, expect that you are going to pick up additional radio traffic and radio skip that could lead some to think the disruption is paranormal.

Coordinate the dates and times of the sightings. If possible, find out when others have experienced paranormal activity and schedule your event for the same time and place. Or schedule the investigation to coincide with the event that you believe is causing the paranormal reporting. Logically, one can only assume the paranormal event would consistently occur within a certain time, specific place, or due to attractive forces such as human intervention, séance, etc.

Secure the site. Ensure the paranormal site is secured by keeping those who would interfere, play a joke or hoax you out of the environment.

Conduct an operational briefing. Make sure all persons involved are assigned meaningful tasks and after the briefing is conducted, have each person brief-back their understanding of what they are to do. This provides group expectations for the individual, accountability, and the basis to provide feedback for improvement.

Use a psychic resource if applicable. If you use a psychic, consider separating your investigation from their walk-through, and then correlate your findings afterwards.

Set up equipment. Place the video, audio, temperature, magnetic, radiation (not often available), and electronic monitoring in effective places where they have the best chance of catching anomalies. Ensure there is an equipment inventory and battery check before everything goes out.

Monitor the readings. When using the equipment, keep your conversations to a minimum. If you do speak while recording, make sure you are articulate and audible enough to not be confused when reviewing the information. Similarly, while on scene, make a note if you hear or see something that might be taken out of context later. Your buddies' footsteps down the hall may turn into an interesting EVP later if you don't make a note at the time.

Slowly input human interactions and communications. Do not let everyone rush into the site at once. Send people in as needed and methodically, constantly monitoring what their presence affects. Interject your interactions and communications slowly. Once all members are inserted into the area and you decide to conclude your monitoring operations, if there is time, you may consider just hanging out for a while. Some people believe simply having humans in the area naturally interacting with one another can stimulate paranormal experiences.

Recover equipment. Ensure an inventory of equipment is completed before leaving the site.

Conduct a team leader debriefing. Key team leaders should quickly (less than five minutes) discuss any problems or important issues before the actual team debriefing. The debriefing should address major issues the team never wants to repeat. If there are none, don't rehash past issues in the team debriefing, simply move forward.

Conduct a team debriefing. This can happen directly after the investigation or if everyone is tired, at a later meeting. In the team debriefing, everyone, one at a time and uninterrupted, goes over what they experienced in the investigation. What their job was, where they were, what they heard and saw, and what they did. This is an essential part of providing an accurate investigation account. By having a clear recount and group understanding of what happened, this step will add to the legitimacy of your claims. It has been my experience that team briefings are more productive if they are held at a later time; briefings directly after an event at 3 AM are often rushed or met with less enthusiasm than briefings planned for when everyone is rested and has time for cool reflection of their experience.

Analyze the gathered data. The lead investigator compiles and goes over all material and observations gathered. In a paranormal group, these duties may be split, but one lead for evidence management is ideal.

Make a determination. Given everything the team has been through and all information that has been gathered, decide about whether the events occur naturally or if they are paranormal.

CASE STUDY: The Ghost Wagon of Westlake Hills, Texas

Through the years, while researching folklore, along with true crime, I have found that stories grow or shrink, remain alone, or mesh together to form what is an indiscernible Frankenstein of half-truths. One of these stories is a tale originating from the rim of the Texas hill country, The Ghost Wagon of Westlake Hills. I heard this tale when I was in elementary school. It told of a ghost man, a ghost dog, a ghost horse, and a ghost wagon that could be seen at dusk, crossing a small stream on Camp Craft Road near Bee Caves, in what was then considered mountainous territory. These days, Westlake Hills is an affluent community southwest of Austin. By car, you can now reach the middle of Westlake Hills from the state capitol building within 15 minutes on a Saturday afternoon. In the late 1800s, it may have taken you an entire day to navigate the rocky terrain, unforgiving vegetation, and steep grades to get near the middle of what is now known as Westlake Hills. At the time of the story, the area was presumed to be known as the homestead of the Marshal Ranch within the now Eanes school district.

Since the 1960s, it has been reported that the ghost wagon originated from a man being killed while he was transporting cotton to Austin at the turn of the century. If that is the case, I commend him. If he was driving a wagon filled with cotton grown in the limestone rocks of the Texas Hill Country, he was not only a cotton farmer but also a magician. But I digress. There was cotton being grown farther west that would likely have been transported over one of the many Lower Colorado River fords leading back into Austin. Whatever or however he was transporting his goods, he was reportedly killed next to a creek and buried there. In *The Big Book of Texas Ghost Stories,* by Alan Brown, it states that the name of the person originally reported to have been killed was Tom Burns. However, the relater of the story then reports the actual name of the man murdered was discovered to be Maurice Moore. Writer Alan Brown's informant, Byron L., is not a historian and was repeating the story the way he remembered it. He had spent much of his youth in that area in the 1960s. Remember, you cannot judge someone responsible for what they don't know. The Byron L. story continues and reports that the man murdered was buried at the ranch along a creek; he was told this by his grandmother when he was very young. In other circulated stories it is said that in the 1960s several kids located skeletal remains in a shallow stream in front of the Eanes Elementary School. Closer to the school is a small graveyard originating from the 1800s; however, locals say there are many unmarked graves in the area. When the children told their parents about the bones, they were informed that the remains were of the cotton farmer Maurice Moore.

Alan Brown was very diligent in his reporting of this story. He notes a discrepancy between the Byron L. story and the historical information he was able to review. Brown could not verify that the driver of the wagon was Maurice Moore, nor would he have been able to, because I know Maurice Moore was not the driver of the wagon. However, Moore was murdered in the same era and in the same area. According to Brown, the driver of the wagon was most likely a man with the surname of Barnes. Where he got this information, I do not know, nor does it matter, because we will now move on.

The following is a historical narrative prepared by the Travis County Sheriff's Office and explains the death of Maurice Moore:

> *During the early morning hours of November 10, 1887, Deputy Maurice "Morris" Moore was shot and killed while serving a civil paper on the McNeil brothers in the Eanes (Marshall) area of Western Travis County. This occurred during an arson investigation of the Eanes Schoolhouse. Deputy Moore discovered that the McNeil brothers had written a letter to the Travis County sheriff confessing to the schoolhouse arson and expressing their desire to surrender. In this letter, the McNeils warned the sheriff not to send Deputy Moore as they would kill him if he tried to apprehend them. Deputy Moore (a former Texas Ranger and man with an unpleasant temperament), married to the Eanes schoolteacher who was the victim of the arson, by happenstance intercepted this letter. Deputy Moore took this warning as a threat and personal challenge and he and an Austin city marshal embarked into the mountain country, as it was called then, to arrest the McNeil brothers with a "Writ of Attachment." The two lawmen camped overnight. Early the next morning, the officers approached the McNeil cabin and tried to gain entry. However, old man McNeil held the officers at bay with a rifle. During the standoff, the Austin marshal tried to disarm old man McNeil while Moore tried to enter the cabin. A shotgun blast from behind the door cut Deputy Moore down and he died instantly.*

The location of this murder may have been several miles to the west, past where the Eanes-Marshal Ranch House now stands, an area that was once known as Moore's Hill. Stories such as these must be validated through private and public records of the incidents. This is where the real investigation lies. Truth be told, there are numerous unmarked graves in the area dating back hundreds of years. There are cemeteries covered by lakes, parks, housing and business developments. Once you begin serious research, you will be surprised what you will find and all that has been forgotten.

As is, the Ghost Wagon of Westlake Hills is an amalgamation of at least four separate stories: (1) the murder of Deputy Sheriff Maurice Moore, (2) the murder of cotton farmer Tom Burns, or a Mr. Barnes, either by Comanche warriors or (3) by highwaymen who sold his wagon team and cotton in Austin, and (4) the sighting of an old man and his dog that kids said they saw disappear like an ghostly phantasm near Moore's Hill.

So, my research begs the question: Did Tom Burns or Mr. Barnes have a dog with him? If so, assuming there was an apparition seen by someone who originated the entire story, does the history of a murder occurring in the area that matches the description of the vision lead to the possibility of a haunting?

I say it does.

CHAPTER 4

The Investigative Process

Paranormal investigations do not have to stand the test of being reviewed by a detective supervisor, a county or district attorney, a grand jury, a judge or jury, but maybe they should be. A true paranormal researcher would not be offended by having their investigation reviewed by their peers; after all, the most important thing in the paranormal quest is to identify the truly paranormal and if a review can help that, investigators should welcome it.

Red Flags
One of the very first skills an investigator needs to develop is the ability to recognize and address mistakes of fact; initial scene assessment and witness qualification are necessities in any investigation. This can be interpreted as recognizing a misunderstanding or identifying a hoax. Never take for granted that the person reporting the paranormal event has their facts right; that is why they call you. Your first responsibility is to identify whether a paranormal investigation is needed.

CASE STUDY: The Three-Girl Possession—Austin, Texas
In 1988, I was assigned as an investigator for the city's mental health unit. At the time, mental health investigators responded to any call in which an organization or individual believed someone was experiencing a mental breakdown and law enforcement intervention was needed. One evening, I received a radio call from the local dispatch advising me that a priest at a local church had called for law enforcement assistance. Patrol officers arrived

and requested the assistance of the mental health unit. When I arrived, the uniformed officer, who sat in his patrol car, rolled down his window and said, "They're inside. Do you need me?" Judging by his tone and demeanor, I made a command decision and told him I didn't. He drove off without another word. This was not at all unusual for patrol officers. Many of them have the mentality that they are there to fight crime and anything secondary to that mission is a distraction. Plus, most simply don't like dealing with emotionally irrational people, especially if they can't just arrest them to solve the problem. I felt it would be better not to have him there.

I entered the church from the side parking lot door and immediately heard a commotion near the back of the church by the altar. I used the shadows and worked my way along the side of the building, walking between the walls and limestone columns that lined the parishioner area. I paused for a moment, observing three girls hysterically crying and a priest trying to calm them and pray with them. After a few seconds, I stepped out of the darkness and introduced myself. One of the girls continued praying and asking for God's forgiveness. The other two were seated on the steps to the altar with the priest sitting beside them. I asked the priest if I could speak with him in his chambers. He got up, ensured the girls that they were safe, and escorted me back behind the altar to a small office that housed extra robes and sacramental items. He explained that the girls had come into the church several hours ago, terrified that a demon was chasing them. All three of the girls were crying and hysterical. I asked the priest if he had seen anything and he said he hadn't. However, he was quick to mention that "something" scared them enough to seek shelter in a church and the solace of a priest. I thanked him and we went to speak with the girls. They were where we had left them, still hysterical, still crying. I walked around them once. I slowly scanned the interior of the church and looked back at them. Two were still praying and one had paused to observe me. When I looked back at her, she looked away and started her prayers again. I asked to speak with her.

She rose to her feet and walked toward me. I turned and walked back to the priest's chambers and he followed. I asked him if he would stay with the other two, to make sure they were okay; he silently agreed. Once back in the little room, I had all the information I required. I just needed confirmation from one of the girls. Because she was distracted by my presence during what they professed was a demonic possession, I knew she would be the one. We stood facing each other, her hands trembling, eyes swollen and red. I asked what happened. She explained they were at one of the other girl's apartment watching a movie and a shadow came into the room. The other girls saw it and they could see its face. It even got onto or in one of the other girls.

She said, "We all saw it. Then the girl started freaking out. We didn't know what to do, so we came straight here; she lives a block down the street."

I paused. I let her hear her own explanation. I let her, in her mind, go over her story again. She was a pleasant looking girl. A nice girl.

I asked her, "Is this the first time you have done this?"

She looked confused but remained silent.

I asked again, "Is this the first time you have done this? You are unnaturally twitchy, rubbing your fingers and thumbs together, your eyes are dilated to the point where I cannot even guess what color they are, and you are seeing things. So, I will ask again, is this the first time you have done this—taken meth?"

Her answer was, "Yes."

My answer was, "Let's not waste any more of this nice priest's time."

We walked back out and I asked the girls if they wanted a ride to the hospital to be checked out or wanted to go home. They all walked home.

Checking the Facts

Initial scene assessment and witness qualification are two of the most important elements of a paranormal investigation. If you allow someone to direct your actions and distract you from isolating the truth, you do yourself and everyone else a great disservice. Fact checking and report corroboration are key elements in establishing the origins of the phenomena.

In retrospect, my handling of the three girls may have been a bit rushed, but that is a perfect example of case management: the ability to compartmentalize your investigation, segregate your responsibilities, and implement the resources at your disposal. I some cases, a chemical induced into the body is what is required for some persons to have clarity of paranormal events or it somehow opens a doorway to another dimension allowing entities to be seen or cross over. However, many of the truly paranormal events reported to law enforcement are brushed off as nothing more than drug induced psychosis. In this case, I would be at fault for handling the three girls the way I did, destroying any chance at investigating the possibilities further. However, because reports like these that come in to law enforcement are typically in an uncontrolled environment, there is no scientific way to prove the paranormal experience over the drug induced one. There are many hypotheses about the girls involved in the Salem Witch Trials. Some believe a psychotropic plant, such as a mushroom or mold, could have affected them and caused them to believe demonic events were occurring. So, until further controlled studies are conducted on the "intoxicant opening the door hypothesis," it will remain unanswered. Unfortunately, if drugs are involved, there must be a dismissal of the paranormal event, unless you discover external evidence.

Methods of Inquiry

There are many ways to conduct an investigation and many independent parts: experiencer information, witness information, location information, physical evidence, latent evidence, and forensics just to name a few. The goal is to get everything covered without influencing or compromising the integrity of the other. For example, when approaching someone about a particular UFO sighting to find out if they saw anything, you would not want to say: "Hello, I am writing a book about the UFO sighting over Snohomish, Washington. You know, the one where thousands of people saw a trail of silver sparks arcing over the mountain just before it crashed." The credibility of whatever you would get from this interview would forever be in question because your approach would be considered "leading the witness." Whenever interviewing anyone, your first go-through should be only what they relay to you.

There are essentially two methods of inquiry, whether you are interviewing for a paranormal event or for a crime: (1) questioning to reconstruct past events, and (2) questioning what, by default, creates new knowledge. The paranormal investigator is not merely investigating a cold case, which is the most difficult of detective tasks, they are also collecting rumors about the event, possible forgeries supporting the event, honest false accounts of the event, and misleading clues of the event, all to unravel the paranormal mystery: What happened and why is something continuing to happen?

Most investigative methods are born from possibilities or facts. In either case, it's up to the investigator to gather enough case information from testimony and evidence to lead a reasonable person to believe a paranormal event occurred. This is usually established by eliminating all the possible, naturally occurring explanations. Whatever is left over should typically remain unknown or an anomaly. Or, in some cases, a true paranormal experience that usually remains unexplained. Here is where methods of investigation and schools of thought differ. So often, this is where the pseudo-scientific approach of using technology to isolate and gather evidence separates from the more humanistic and spiritual approach. Is your goal (1) to eliminate naturally occurring events and locate and record a phenomenon using technology, or is your goal (2) to locate and communicate with other entities using a medium or humanistic approach? Or is it both? There are some who think that the spiritual connection with anyone in the afterlife is a psychic ability that some people possess. That phenomena perceived by experiencers is only apparent to those experiencing the connection and would not be detected through technology. This could be considered what I call a dimensional perception of the entity or an event seen only by those with minds open to such things.

So, in developing your investigative methods, establish a standard protocol in which other investigative groups can come behind you and essentially perform the same investigative measures, and in theory, get the same results.

Understanding and Determining Your Methods

In most paranormal cases, investigators receive a claim that a property is haunted. They take the statement from the reportee, look online to vet the report (because everything you read online is true...), set a time to go over to investigate it, go over, set up their equipment, observe for a couple of hours, and call it a night. That is not an investigation—that is a reconnaissance. That is an initial survey. An investigation is an examination of all parts of the puzzle, not just catching the lamp flicker on video. Not just capturing the orb over grandma's favorite china cabinet. Do not get me wrong, I get it; most of the people involved in investigating such claims are volunteers with a limited amount of time to devote to the process. I've been there. The problem is that the paranormal entity is not working on your time schedule. That is why the vetting of the witness or reportee and the initial research on the site location is so important. If you simply take every story at face value and run off into the sunset, the likelihood of discovering one truly unexplained event goes down. Yes, it goes down. Some would argue that the more fishhooks you have in the water, the more fish you will catch. That may be true with fishing, but it has nothing to do with locating a truly paranormal event. If you allow people to waste your time chasing rabbits, you will have less time chasing ghosts. Paranormal investigations are about conducting the initial research. They are about culling out all the restaurant and bar owners that want to hang the haunted sign on their doors for more business. They are about eliminating the crackpot who wants attention or the truly psychotic person who is off medication and channeling nothing more than a flight of delusional ideas. Investigation is about 80 percent preparation and 20 percent on-scene exploration. It is about discovering the solutions that allow long-term, undisturbed observation of the suspected area. It is about all the non-sexy steps needed for a true case study. A case study culminating the entire breadth of the investigation, not just the Electronic Voice Phenomena (EVP) picked up on someone's recorder.

Like law enforcement, paranormal investigations have certain steps that should be addressed in every case. The purpose of law enforcement investigations is to identify the guilty and eliminate the innocent. Conviction and restitution are up to the courts. In paranormal investigations, it is the investigator's responsibility to identify the phenomena and eliminate human and other natural causes. This is done through a series of logical arguments using inductive or deductive reasoning:

Inductive reasoning. This deals with having strong evidence that a person's premise about a thing or idea is true. As an example, we can say the upstairs of Buffalo Billiards in Austin, Texas is a hot spot for paranormal events base on the facts that:

1. The building was a doctor's office where many people died
2. Orbs and other phenomena have been recorded
3. There was no identified external light to cause the experience

Therefore, it is probable that the bar is haunted because of the presence of orbs. In many cases, that is the way inductive reasoning works in the paranormal industry.

Deductive reasoning. This is a more concrete form of reasoning and requires more grounded examples of the reasoning steps. Deduction starts with an assumed theory, such as: light spectrum anomalies and dust cause orbs in camera equipment. From that premise, one can begin by eliminating any possibility of ambient light affecting the camera lens equipment and shutting down ventilation well prior to the beginning of the investigation. Once this is eliminated and orbs continue to plague the equipment, one can deduce the possibly that something paranormal is revealing itself to investigators. Valid deductive arguments follow the initial known rule, not an assumption.

Refining Your Investigative Procedure

One of the hardest things to determine in a paranormal investigation is whether or not the reported event ever occurred. The initial report should be investigated, if possible. In child abuse, this would be called the outcry statement. It is the child's first report to an adult that some sort of inappropriate behavior occurred. Here I will refer to it as the paranormal alpha report. This first report will originate from the first person to witness the phenomenon to the first person they tell. How is this important, you ask? It will provide an origin of the event and will allow investigators to more critically examine the circumstances behind the report and the motivation for reporting the incident to another person. In many older cases, the alpha report will exist only in a newspaper article or some sort of written record. This will be considered the incident's alpha report; even though the original person experiencing the phenomenon is not noted.

A good example of this is the original April 17, 1897, *Dallas Morning News* article written by S. E. Haden, titled: "A Windmill Demolishes It." The article recounts how a slow-moving silver aircraft crashed into a local resident's windmill and exploded, killing the pilot and leaving his body burned and wreckage strewn about. His remains were described as not of this world and possibly of the planet Mars. Oddly enough, there was never a follow-up article of this incident nor were there private or governmental records recording the event or the event of the pilot's burial. Much later, two people came forward as witnesses to seeing the craft; however, there was no additional corroborating evidence or testimony. Later, research suggests that due to a series of unfortunate circumstances, Aurora, Texas was on the verge of collapse and this report may have been an attempt to garner attention and stimulate tourism for the economy. For a time, there was a marker where it was said the pilot was buried. However, serious research into the evidence was met with resistance and unfortunately, most serious investigators have lost interest.

After giving a lecture at the 2014 Michigan Paranormal Conference, I had three people come by my booth to share UFO experiences with me. Two happened to be licensed professionals, the other one was a person off their medication. Sorry, I was a mental health officer; I recognized the signs and symptoms of diagnosed psychosis. Of the two professionals, both asked that I not reveal their names. Realizing the precarious nature of their reports as related to their occupations, I did not delve into the specifics of their encounters. However, I find it increasingly interesting how many people want to share their experiences with me, once they find out I am a researcher of the subject. Of my two professionals, one had a child with her at the time of the encounter and the other was alone. Both denied substance abuse or a mental health history, and both described similar experiences. A large, oval, metallic craft with lights, no noise, and a "here it is, now it's gone" event. Both said the lights were brighter than anything they have ever seen, and both swore, based on their understanding of air and spacecraft, the objects were not of this world. This is what is referred to in law enforcement as a "no leads case." I have nothing to investigate. No additional witnesses to interview (that I know of), no apparent physical evidence to recover or analyze, and no involved suspects to contact. Even to go back to the event location and search for other witnesses at this point would be rather useless, for the simple fact that it would be too difficult to correlate the event to the time and place, and both had occurred over 10 years ago. Gathering more witness information is interesting; however, that still does not prove the event occurred; it just makes for a more interesting legend. We want quality over quantity.

In refining your investigative process, you must determine what is and what is not crucial to your investigation. When investigating an arrested burglar, it is common to look into their associates to determine how many other burglaries they have committed, where and to whom they fence the property, and establish who is involved. That's what the academy says to do. That's what the books tell you to do. In reality, if a detective were to follow up on all the leads from a comprehensive burglary case, he could spend the rest of his career making case after case based just on the leads from that one report. It's called "going down the rabbit hole."

How Thorough is Complete?

For a professionally employed investigator to take cases, day after day, he must understand the flow: (1) to investigate the leads to an offense, (2) develop probable cause, (3) file for the arrest, and (4) move on to the next case. A great example of this is the incredible work that Don Schmitt and Tom Carey have done in their book *Witness to Roswell* (2009). As a professional investigator, I am completely mind-boggled over the extent of these two men's search for answers. They have interviewed hundreds upon hundreds of people involved, claiming to be involved, or claiming to have information related to people who claimed to be involved. They have travelled across the country and spent countless hours researching and documenting their finds. I have the utmost respect for them and Stanton Friedman for their dedication to one of the Air Force's most baffling cover-ups; and it was a cover up. Something did happen. With that said, considering the case of human psychology and contemporary logic, one can only take in so much unfettered information. An investigator cannot take a quantitative approach to determining facts. More information is not necessarily better. A qualitative approach to investigations is what is usually required. A few hard facts and physical evidence will trump hearsay and speculation every time.

Defining the parameters and limits to your investigation is the key to managing the case and refining your investigative process. And your process will become more refined with experience; along the way, you will learn to recognize quality.

CHAPTER 5
Quality of Information

In many cases, the source for the paranormal report will enjoy being a part of the entire investigative process. When this is the case, ensure you provide them credit for their part and for the information they have brought forward. Include them, when possible, in the investigative and documentation process. I have been a witness to attention-seeking ghost hunters who would ultimately eliminate the initial person who came forward with the experience and then relay the story as if it were their own or as a story passed down. This behavior creates mistrust within the community and will get you ostracized rather quickly with your peers.

If your source wishes to remain anonymous, honor their wishes and take extraordinary measures to ensure their identity is not compromised.

Controversy
One of the most powerful things to understand is that controversial subjects always create the most polarizing opinions, and paranormal subjects are controversial. Therefore, we can all expect to be exposed to expressive and emotional responses from those involved. In order to combat such confrontations, participants need to approach the specific investigation with a level of decorum that facilitates a productive environment. You need to decide whether it's worth arguing about menial things, such as moving a trash can from one side of the desk to the other because one person is left

handed and the other is right. The trash can is still in the room. Is whatever you are disputing really that important in the overall scheme of the investigation and the outcome? As explained by Rosemary Ellen Guiley in *The Djinn Connection* (2013), investigators can easily confuse naturally occurring phenomena for paranormal, and a haunting or shadow people experience with Djinn activity, or something else. It takes daunting dedication and documentation to identify the root of the experience. It also takes patience and the avoidance of trivial matters.

Objectivity

When scientifically investigating the unexplained, the supernatural, or the paranormal, investigators cannot be too objective. Remaining objective for a paranormal researcher can be difficult at times. Many paranormal researchers are inherently subjective, led by their personal feelings, beliefs, and opinions while trying to prove the existence of the other side. They dedicate personal and family time, money and energy, subjecting themselves to danger, scrutiny, and ridicule for something they believe in and desire to prove. At times this lends itself to assisting the inner desire of the investigator to become true. Like overzealous police, more than one paranormal investigator has had to answer for research inconsistencies ranging from simple exaggerations to outright hoaxes. Despite the investigator's beliefs, feelings, interpretations, or prejudices, remaining objective and dealing with only the things external to personal beliefs should be the ultimate goal. But therein lies the problem: what if perceiving hauntings, possessions, shadow people and the like require the human mind, the psyche, in order to be seen, detected, or observed?

Coincidence

Detectives often say there is no such thing as a coincidence. Always be wary of coincidental occurrences when researching, interviewing, and investigating the paranormal. In most cases, these situations will reveal themselves. In his book *Blink,* author and researcher Malcolm Gladwell discusses the strange reasons we know certain unexplainable things. Conclusions we seem to gather from feelings rather than conventional information. While you cannot rely entirely on your instincts or intuition, any red flag should be noted and researched extensively; there is a reason your brain keyed in on the topic. Explore it and trust your feelings.

Managing Bias

In every situation, investigators must deal with bias. Oddly enough, many paranormal investigators have very strong biases toward paranormal events other than the ones they investigate. Some ghost hunters do not believe in UFOs, and vice versa. Some cryptozoologists do not believe in demons, and so on. Whatever the true answer is, the main issue is that you, as an investigator, must maintain neutrality in your bias by simply conducting good research and good fieldwork that you and your peers can examine and decide upon.

Classifying Information

When investigating, a good detective never ignores potential sources of information or clues. However, after careful examination they know how to categorize the information: (1) relevant / related, (2) relevant / unrelated, (3) not relevant.

1. Relevant / Related: This is information, testimony, or evidence that is relevant to the event being investigated and related to the described phenomena.

EXAMPLE: Information that a male apparition was seen at the location of a murdered male.

2. Relevant / Unrelated: This is information, testimony, or evidence that is relevant to a paranormal event but cannot be attributed to a specific cause.

EXAMPLE: Orbs seen at the location of a murder.

3. Not relevant: This is information, testimony, or evidence that does not relate to the confirmation or denial of any paranormal event.

EXAMPLE: Urban legend or intentionally false or misleading information.

Remember, any information you gather will come from one or more of the following sources: (1) people, (2) physical evidence, and (3) documented records.

Case Screenings and Previous Investigations

To understand investigations, you need to study investigations. By reviewing or screening other investigators' work and breaking down their methods and processes, you can get a clear picture of their approach to the problem and identify biases and weaknesses in their methods. We all have them. In law enforcement, there is always the looming threat that if they want you, they can get you. That is, if your supervisors or the administration wants to stop your progress, they can, simply by reviewing your work. Every investigator will have weaknesses, and every investigation will too. Due to the overwhelming caseload of most law enforcement departments, it is practically impossible to thoroughly investigate every case. I can assure you, anyone can look through a case file and ask why you didn't do this or do that. However, that is how we learn to become better at what we do. We learn from our shortcomings, but preferably from others.

The methods and processes an investigator uses in a case are far more important than the outcome of that investigation. The TV show *Uncovering Aliens* features four proclaimed expert UFO investigators: Maureen Elsberry, Steven Jones, Mike Bara, and Derrel Sims. I apologize now, but I feel I have to say this. This show is a good example of how to not conduct an investigation—show editing has a lot to do with this. While the premise of the show had promise, the fact that the investigators are not experienced with many of the tools used was readily apparent. Also, the fact that they confuse causations of biologically occurring evidence and human stress behavior, misidentification of satellites and meteors, and create actual testimonial fabrications, should lead real aspiring investigators to steer clear of their techniques. In defense of the investigators, we can assume that they were asked or required to perform certain actions for the show for the sake of drama.

At one point in Episode 2, Derrel says it is possible that some radiation may have been knocked off a spacecraft that had been shot at with a shotgun.

Think about that for a moment. The spaceship survived travelling light years through time and space, through a debris-littered galaxy only to get shot with a redneck's scatter gun and have some of its radiation knocked off? Dang the luck. By the way, I love Derrel, so please don't get my intention wrong. It's just that when presenting a hypothesis, make sure your assessment is factual.

So, I would like to cover three examples, just to show you how little things can cause huge gaps in your investigation.

Example one. During *Uncovering Aliens* Episode 3, researching alien harvesting, aeronautics engineer Mike Bara hypothesizes that the claimed abductee experienced missing time due to lighting strikes in the area when the alleged abduction occurred. His theory is that a close lightning strike can cause memory loss and did so in this case. To prove his point, he performs a rudimentary rote memory test on Maureen, then convinces her to don a metal mesh suit and exposes her to 750,000 volts of direct current electricity. Afterward, he performs his memory test again, and she did, in fact, have decreased memory after the exposure to electricity. While there is no doubt that conventional common sense would lead a person to believe that someone suffering an electrical shock could be affected by loss of memory, the fact remains that anyone, under any acute duress or stress, has noticeable loss of memory. In this case, the 750,000 volts of direct current was not the cause. Simple fear and a natural fight-or-flight response has been proven to cause loss or delay of memory. The point is, if an experiment cannot isolate the cause of an event, why do it? Also, in this case, they conducted the experiment and then researched the Weather Bureau to discover there was no lighting in the area at the time of the abduction. Now, I will give Mike the benefit of the doubt and say that the show's director wanted to do the experiment anyway, regardless of its appropriateness, because it was cool watching Maureen squirm. I understand the TV stuff.

Example two. Again, in Episode 3, Steven Jones interviews Timothy Good, a UFO authority in the United Kingdom. During the interview, Good confirms that he has a reliable Washington source that affirms "a hybridization program is in process" by a group of aliens that are intent in taking over the planet. These programs are being conducted in underground and underwater bases. Steven then asks who knows about this and Good clearly says, "If there was one prime minister, I would say Margaret Thatcher, because she got to know Reagan very well...Reagan himself had been briefed on the alien situation. I am quite sure he would have discussed it with Margaret Thatcher." Steven turns right around and summarizes that Good told him that Maggie Thatcher knew about this (the hybrid program). It is little statements like this that mislead juries and mislead the public on controversial topics such as this, and damage whatever legitimacy there may be in the investigation. Once an investigator is shown to fabricate anything within the scope of their investigation, the rest of the information and evidence becomes suspect to nothing more than a guess and the entire investigation can be discredited.

Example three. This is the "Underwater Alien Base" episode in which Derrel dons standard scuba equipment and goes for a dive in Lake Michigan to discover a hidden underwater UFO installation. I meet the qualifications of a master scuba diver, have been trained as a rescue diver in Alaska, was assigned to a law enforcement underwater recovery team, and have over 70 hours of what would be considered as "black water" scuba experience, so I can assure you this venture may have been the single biggest waste of TV airtime of all the *Uncovering Aliens* endeavors. Not only are there inexpensive detection technologies to locate underwater structures but also the depth of the water for a normal air breathing scuba diver is limited (to approximately 120 feet – safely with very limited bottom-time), which makes this project pointless. Not to mention the fact that Lake Michigan's average depth is 279 feet and covers a surface area of approximately 22,300 square miles, close to the entire size of the state of West Virginia. It was like watching Geraldo Rivera's infamous special report on Al Capone's vault, all over again. Nothing... nothing...and nothing. You simply cannot maintain credibility conducting such disorganized and poorly thought-out searches and investigations, even if it is for the TV producers.

When conducting a case screening, one should, at minimum:

1. Identify the correct time and date of the original event.
2. Identify the correct time and date of the subsequent event(s).
3. Identify all possible locations connected with the event.
4. Identify all location histories.
5. Identify all possible persons connected to the event.
6. Identify all personal histories.
7. Identify all physical evidence.
8. Identify all phenomena observed, past and current.
9. Identify any methods or experiments the investigators conduct.
10. Determine if their methods uncovered what they intended to uncover.

By conducting a thorough investigation and a comprehensive review of previous inquiries by both conventional investigators and paranormal specialists, you will be better prepared to take the next step in identifying entity behavior.

CHAPTER 6

Event Orienting and Identification

To establish the cause of an event, your organization of information is essential. It is useful to gather as much evidence as possible, and categorize the event using dates, times, the physical events (orbs, footsteps, etc.), methods of observation, natural explanations, and unexplained phenomena. Once you have identified specific topics of examination you can begin to correlate common relationships between the topics defined.

Behavior Patterns

You should always attempt to "profile" the entity. In doing so, you will begin to identify what is called, in contemporary law enforcement investigations, the modus operandi (MO) for the phenomena. As an example, the Eanes-Marshall Ranch House in West Lake Hills, Texas has reported phenomena of footsteps being heard from upstairs. The cause of the footsteps is unknown, the times are random, and there is no recorded death in the building. But that would be the definable and consistent event that reoccurs. Some places are known for orbs, some for whispers, and some for apparitions, etc. The point of what I call Phenomena Pattern Analysis (PPA) is to define combinations of events in order to recreate and identify why they are occurring. PPA is a classification method used to identify specific characteristics related to anomalistics.

Most everything that remains consistent has a pattern. Investigators conduct their inquiry in a particular way in order to ensure that everything they need to cover is done, time and time again. Criminals who specialize in particular crimes also develop a certain way they conduct their business, their MO or mode of operation. You, as a paranormal investigator, need to develop an MO, one that fits your time constraints, physical and mental abilities, and one that will remain consistent and stand up to peer review. While criminals may intentionally change their MO, those of the paranormal nature should remain consistent. This is your opportunity to create your own system and branch away from the methods of other paranormal researchers. A poorly researched and carelessly conducted hunt could result in condemnation from the paranormal community. Craft your investigation style in order to avoid this.

Keeping Track

In the last decade of ghost hunting TV shows, to the best of my knowledge, no one has been able to capture a ghost, physically. However, the electronic interpretations of mechanical sensors and audio and video depictions of exceptional events have been captured. These sets of data can be reviewed for analysis. In doing so, while managing paranormal investigations, one must create some form or model in which to categorize measurable criteria. Using what I call the Isolating Paranormal Incidents (IPI) model, one can easily set up a spreadsheet to record, tally, and categorize statistical data and create a basis of evaluation. Here is an example of a list of generalized topics in no particular order:

1. Number of paranormal events reported
2. Number of paranormal events investigated
3. Number of paranormal events resulting in no activity
4. Number of paranormal events resulting in explained activity
5. Number of paranormal events resulting in unexplained activity
6. Number of paranormal events identifying paranormal activity
7. Full body apparition
8. Partial apparition
9. Glow, mist, or distortion(s)
10. Orb(s)
11. Shadow(s)

12. Mechanism of Paranormal Indicators (items moving)
13. Temperature changes
14. Tactile experiences
15. Intuition / gut feeling / insight

Managing the investigation is about managing time, allotting responsibility and resources, and gathering data. Oh, and it's about arriving at a conclusion, don't forget that one. Everyone will want to know what you have uncovered and what you think.

Case Management

Managing your investigation is a task in and of itself. Staying on track and following the relevant clues are real challenges. Oftentimes, you cannot tell which findings are relevant and which are not. That is where experience and instinct play a key part. In some cases, there are simply too many trails to follow, too much "helpful" information from the others, and too many unknowns. In some cases, you must let it go.

EXAMPLE: Sadomasochist Sex Ring—Austin, Texas

While investigating a report of multiple sex crimes involving several individuals and one primary suspect, I was faced with a real challenge: (1) continue chasing phantoms down the rabbit hole, or (2) know when to give up and move on. For some that is an easy proposition, to keep working and go get the bad guy. As an officer of the law, it's not that easy. Cases don't stop coming because you are buried deep in a complex one. In this incidence, the crimes happened over several years, and the last event occurred two months prior to the initial report. There were multiple people, organizations, and locations involved. The person initially reporting the crime had a manipulative personality and previously had multiple conversations with the people who were eventually identified as victims.

There were credibility issues involved with the reportee and victims, and illegal drug involvement. Once I began my research on the persons involved, I realized that every one of them had multiple things to hide and reasons to not be entirely honest with law enforcement. Of the locations involved, several were, I believe, intentionally sold by the owners after the investigation was initiated. And because the individuals involved were no longer the owners of these locations, I did not have enough probable cause to obtain search warrants to discover any evidence the suspect(s) may have been concealing there. In my last efforts, I went to one of the most promising locations and contacted the new owners. I explained what I believed the location was used for and requested that they consent to my searching the property for evidential signs that the acts were committed on the premises. They smiled and politely refused.

A few days later my original reportee was arrested on unrelated charges. A few weeks later, video reviews of the original interviews of the victims showed strong evidence of coaching on the part of the reportee to influence the victim's testimony and make sure they were all on the same page. In this case, the true question began to surface: even if I find what I believe is the truth, will I be able to prove it? In my case, prove it in court. With all the cross contaminated coached testimony of the supposed victims, the contradictory eyewitness accounts from the public, and the lack of physical evidence associated with the suspect, I let the case go and suspended it indefinitely; unfounded. That is what you may have to do with much of your work investigating the paranormal; let it go as unsolved.

To be clear, your process of investigation is more important than the outcome of your investigation. Do your research and follow your leads. If you do it in a methodical and ethical way, your investigation will stand on its own and will be useful to others who come behind you and try it again.

And again.

Rely on sound investigative foundations.

CHAPTER 7

Investigative Foundations

The investigative process is not a step-one, step-two, step-three process. Investigation is a means to an end: discovering the truth about an event. We are truth-seekers. However, there are always basic rules or guidelines anyone in any type of investigation should follow:

General Investigative Rules

1. Do not violate the law unless you are willing to accept the consequences. The primary law paranormal investigators break on a routine basis is Criminal Trespass. Because of restricted public access to private property, many investigators take it upon themselves to risk arrest to gain this access. If you chose this route, at least have a good local bondsman.

2. Know your subject. Do your research before conducting your onsite investigation. It doesn't work to find yourself searching for signs of a ghost when you are dealing with an occult occurrence or something demonic.

3. Be honest with all your sources of information. There may be a time, when conducting historical research, that you should avoid sharing with your source that you are ghost hunting. It may be beneficial to remain as an amateur historian, and you are.

4. Seek the facts equally from people whom you do not like, and those you do; facts have nothing to do with favoritism.

5. Avoid politics; affiliations can influence your outcome. Be careful.

6. Use only direct evidence when determining your conclusion about an event. Bottom line, you either have evidence, or you don't. If you don't, and your background research supports the need for evidence, then more investigation is needed. If the investigation is a true ghost hunt, then it might be time to close the case.

7. Avoid any exaggeration or distortion of the evidence in your investigation.

Understanding Multiple Perspectives

Whenever anyone tries to identify the specifics of a particular subject, there will be those who will argue the validity of those specifics. When I was conducting my internship for my law enforcement agency's range master position (firearms program manager), I learned a great deal from my predecessor, Lawrence Salas. It is interesting how truly good teachers rarely supply their students with the answer; they usually just pose additional questions. One day I was straightening what was the range office, a 10x10-foot backyard storage shed. It had a set of shelves, a desk, a box of ear protector headsets, scattered boxes of ammunition, and other assorted things used for firearms training and qualification. It was an incredibly inept facility for an agency of over 1,000 gunslingers. One day, I decided to move the trash can to the other side of the desk, because I thought, being closer to where we issued ammunition, I could more easily discard the empty ammo boxes. Then I thought it would be good to move the hearing protection to the shelf, so I could more easily hand the headsets to shooters. Then I moved the sign-in book to the shelf near the door so the shooters could sign in at the door instead of cluttering up the "office" by entering and crowding up at the desk. Lawrence looked at me and suggested that we move the desk to the other side of the 10x10-foot space to create more room at the entryway, and hang the hearing protection on nails on the wall, and put the sign-in book outside on the inspection table, and get two trash cans, one for the right side of the desk and one for the left side, etc., etc., etc. The more suggestions he gave, the bigger his grin. I sat down and shut up; there is only so much you can do with a 10x10-foot shed.

There are many ways to conduct the same evolution, many different methods to elicit the same outcome. In the world of paranormal investigation, one of the challenges is choosing an industry standard method and sticking to it. The end goal of creating a framework for your credibility is repeatability. Even if everything in the situation is subjective, the goal is to have someone repeat your steps up to the place where the objectivity becomes subjectivity and then say, "What evidence did you get that was different from mine?" As challenging as sticking to a standard is, the real challenge is to be flexible, to recognize what you are being flexible on, and to be able to confidently explain why you adjusted the method. With a clear understanding of the arguments, oversights, and deviations in your techniques, much of the controversy can be diverted. Ultimately, the point is to gather the relevant information.

Be aware, investigative rules will differ from specific investigation to specific investigation. When searching for a rapist, law enforcement officers must be well versed in victimology in order to obtain the best information from the victim. On top of that specific skill set, they should also be able to pull from their tool belts the foundation skills of arrest, search and seizure law stemming from the Fourth Amendment, avoiding Mirandizing the suspect too early in the investigation, and limiting a detective's questioning abilities. Hauntings, possession, UFO, and cryptid investigations also have their unique "investigative rules" which are not always initially definable.

Investigative Etiquette

While investigative rules may change, investigative etiquette does not. Care must be taken with all persons involved. The investigative etiquette remains similar in most cases, whether it is related to law enforcement or paranormal events. Investigative etiquette can be maintained by (1) remaining professional with everyone you interact with in your investigation, (2) avoiding territorial confrontations with others in the field and in your group, and (3) being supportive in ways that advance the paranormal field and your own investigations. Follow these three guidelines and you will be an asset to paranormal research as a whole.

As in many situations and many such occupations, there will be rivalry. Law enforcement is pitted with it. However, there is a difference. For law enforcement officers, upholding the law is their job. They are given a badge and granted authority in their jurisdiction, and they are usually the final defining factor in an investigation. On the other hand, paranormal investigators have no legitimate authority under which they operate and no jurisdictions. Paranormal investigators and their teams must maintain a higher level of professionalism in order to prove their competency. You cannot build a sound reputation as a professional investigator by degrading others. You cannot, in the long term, establish a supportive clientele reference base by demeaning others. You cannot establish credibility as a proficient researcher by disparaging others. Avoid these pitfalls at all costs. They will not positively influence your goals and will ultimately define you as a gossip-monger and a whiner. Through individual experience, clients learn to avoid those types and eventually they quit calling, and the team members eventually quit showing up.

I have seen and heard many members of rival teams talk about the other team's lack of experience or the ineffectual ways in which they conduct their investigations. But remember, if we all investigated in the same manner, what are we missing by not branching out and trying new things and experimenting with new techniques? Paranormal investigators do not have to agree with an individual or with group methods, but we must be supportive of the paranormal investigation or we will destroy ourselves from within.

Analysis of Investigative Efforts

Typically, there is a lot of competition in the workplace. Whether it is between corporate rivals or government entities, competition can be a source of motivation or a cause of destructive attacks and dirty politics. Spend your very valuable time on productive things that matter. Should it be that you review another person's or a team's work on a paranormal subject, review it in a positive, objective way that will lead to additional understanding, not in an emotionally destructive way that is completely discrediting.

When I work patrol, I am one of those cops who get out of their car a lot and walk around. I check under bridges, abandoned houses, condemned properties, restricted governmental lands, and other places where you would not expect a patrol officer to go. I do not sit on a busy thoroughfare running radar all day long and writing tickets. I do not sit and watch stop signs, or monitor school zones, or look for expired registration or inspection stickers. But all these things are law enforcement's responsibility. If all cops did their job the same way, many things would be overlooked. Like the body of the missing elderly person I found along the lakeshore nearly two years after he was reported missing. Or the dead man I found sitting in his recliner in what appeared to be an abandoned trailer house. Or the three methamphetamine labs I discovered in small shacks off in the woods. Like law enforcement, there needs to be a diversity of professional, paranormal approaches to investigations. If all paranormal investigators worked from the same handbook, we would be overlooking a lot of anomalies that need explaining.

Cooperative Critique

When reviewing someone else's work, do so professionally, in a way to advance mutual understanding. If you find yourself getting caught up in potential mudslinging, or disputes with those who rival you, move on. Concentrate your time on your projects and the persons who support you. Bickering with people who are, in the big picture, inconsequential to you, is a waste of your emotions and resources. Time is your most important resource. You cannot get it back.

Be the professional you would expect others to be. This will eventually get you to the truth.

PART TWO
The Interview

CHAPTER 8
Digging Up the Truth

Much like the rest of the investigation, the interview has some general guidelines influenced by gut feeling, intuition, and experience in dealing with people and understanding their behavior. While many investigators strive to seek out additional training and methods of conducting interviews and interrogations through steps and techniques, others are just naturally adept at it. Many of those I know who are naturally adept at interrogation typically have core fundamental personality disorders. This is true. If assessed by a psychologist they would have a type A personality, are narcissists, and may even have borderline sociopathic tendencies. This means that they like to take charge of a situation, want everyone else to know they are absolutely the best person to oversee the situation, and are willing to do whatever it takes to convict the guilty person.

Those labels don't sound so bad when you put them in context with getting the job done. I know these facts because (1) I was going to get my degree in psychology before I realized I didn't want to hear others' problems, and (2) I worked very closely with these people and knew them well; personality disorders abound within law enforcement. These particular individuals' intuition stemmed from their internal voicing of what they would like to do in a situation and what they actually decide to do. They identify what they would like to do, and project that onto the person being interviewed. The good criminal interviewer often walks a thin line between interview and interrogation.

However, an effective paranormal investigator gathers information while building a relationship with the witness. If discrepancies, inconsistencies, or lies surface during the interview, cross-examination of the conflicting information may be in order; however, it is highly unlikely for a paranormal investigator to conduct an interrogation of a witness. Gaining their trust and cooperation is the true key.

EXAMPLE: Poorly scripted interview—Austin, Texas

One afternoon, I was the only detective in the office. I was taking time to catch up on my paperwork since there were no distractions. After several hours, I heard on the police radio several officers responding to a burglary call. The suspects were seen, chased, and caught. After about an hour, the suspects were brought through my office and placed into our two interview rooms. Several more minutes went by and another detective asked if I would sit in on his interview with the suspects. I obliged and went in with him. There, seated in a small plastic chair in the corner of the room, was an 18-year-old, would-be copper thief. I sat in a chair along the wall; the interviewing detective sat in the chair in front of the suspect. The detective immediately introduced himself and me, explained why he was being arrested, and then read him his Miranda Rights:

(1) You have the right to remain silent, (2) Anything you say can and will be used against you in a court of law, (3) You have the right to talk to a lawyer and have him present with you while you are being questioned, (4) If you cannot afford to hire a lawyer, one will be appointed to represent you before any questioning if you wish, and (5) You can decide at any time to exercise these rights and not answer any questions or make any statements.

Once completed, the suspect did not decline to talk, so the detective opnotepad and read prewritten questions to him. One through 10. Were you alone? Did you steal the copper? Who was driving the car? Have you been arrested before? And so on until he completed his list of questions. The situation was awkward at best. Then he said, "I am going to give you the opportunity to tell me anything you wish to tell me. Do you want to tell me anything I haven't already asked you?" The suspect said, "No, I wasn't there." That was the end of the interview. The failure of this detective was in his delivery. He seemed dispassionate, robotic, and read from his notes; it was a waste of time. Ultimately, no charges were not filed in this case, however the suspect was later arrested on other crimes resulting from the incident (business receipts obtained from a local copper recycler). Had the detective sat down, developed a dialogue with the suspect, included his questions informally in the dialogue, and had previously gathered factual information so he could cross examine the suspect's inconsistencies and lies, the result would have been different.

Communication is Personal

An interview is a personal thing—a human thing. That detective should have entered the room and attempted to create an environment comfortable for an unobtrusive, normal conversation and behavior observation. He should have mixed his interview with normal things, the weather, sports, cars, movies, anything other than looking down at his pad while reciting preformed queries. If the suspect is untruthful in the conversation, the interrogation can come later. As a paranormal investigator, it will be very unlikely that you will ever have to interrogate someone, but with proper understanding, you will certainly informally cross-examine every witness to ensure you have their facts correct.

Earning Cooperation

In most criminal cases, the suspect will deny his involvement. In paranormal cases, some witnesses will be pleased to be interviewed, some will be skeptical of the interview because they don't want to share personal experiences, and some simply don't want to look crazy; these are considered reluctant witnesses. It is your job as the interviewer to address any objections in a positive light. You need to honor the reportee's wishes, even if that means their refusal to allow you to use their real name. As you know, without a reportee who will be willing to swear to a paranormal experience, you just have another ghost story. And, sometimes that's all you have, and that's okay. Some people will completely refuse to "go on the record." That does not mean you give up. You continue gathering the information, and you continue cultivating a relationship with them. Maybe one day, you will build enough trust with this person, and they will be willing to affirm their story.

Canvassing the Area

When investigating an occurrence that should have been seen by or is known by many people, such as a giant metallic orb hovering in the sky over a populated area or a widely known haunting, you may want to canvass that area looking for more leads. This can be conducted as a door-to-door search, or talking with people in the local diner, other businesses, a civic center, or other gathering places. Notice I wrote, "talking with," not "to." One of the biggest failures of law enforcement investigators is that they talk too much and don't listen enough.

In some cases, when investigating occurrences at a specified location, you may run into people who live in the area, or you may hear additional talk about an occurrence. This information often comes from what would be considered the unaware witnesses. Canvassing often identifies them, and without canvassing, you never would have obtained the information. These are people who experienced something they did not attribute to the paranormal: sounds in a house, lights in the woods, or touches in an empty room. These types of people are usually skeptical of the paranormal, and they typically talk themselves out of the event they experienced, believing it unremarkable, or completely dismissing it. In any case, gathering information they consider insignificant may further your investigation later. Make sure you tell them to hold nothing back. Something they consider insignificant may later prove to be the most important piece of information you have.

Interview Locations

The interview location is important. In some cases, a good investigator will have multiple interview locations: (1) a restaurant for the initial story, (2) a walkthrough of the incident location, (3) in the car while driving to different areas, (4) at the person's home, and (5) in an environment completely controlled by the investigator. The person you are interviewing will have slightly different emotional responses to each location. They will recall different things to expound on at each location. People are comfortable in their own environment; they feel they are in control. Once out of their environment, their speech is less controlled, they are actively observing the environment, and they point out things they would never comment on if your interview was conducted at their kitchen table.

Memory Retrieval

There are so many things that affect memory. Entire books have been written dedicated to identifying and understanding memory. The one thing to remember is that memory is flexible and changes over time. Like muscles, memory needs exercise. Imagine your memories being bridges made of proteins. They connect different parts and images of the memory with other parts. Without maintenance, these bridges will crumble and collapse. If you do not regularly retrieve and review your memories, they will fade over time. Also, in some cases, memory proteins break down, and when you review that old memory, the tendency is to fill in the gaps of the missing portion of that memory with what you believe would have been there based on your knowledge of the event and persons, places, and things in it. Yes, your memory changes. According to Daniela Schiller, of Mt. Sinai School of Medicine, memories are malleable constructs that are reconstructing with each recall. Often thought of as being like Swiss cheese, Schiller describes memories more like processed cheese; more and more things are added. What we remember changes each time we recall the event. Understand that many of these changes may be quite small and insignificant, but over time, memory change can be very pronounced.

Witness Misinterpretations

Also, do not discount any physical conditions your witness may have. Lower cognitive functioning and physical abnormalities of the eyes, ears, nose, and touch can lead to errors in their comprehension of an event. As an example, people who have had eye surgery may suffer from aberrations (irregularities) in their vision in the form of white spots called "floaters" and halos. These new visions can be turned into a paranormal event when in fact it was all in their head. These floaters can appear in broad daylight and resemble floating balls of white light. Halos are most often seen at night and often surround illuminated objects, or objects in a dark area that are reflecting ambient light.

Asking questions such as these builds your credibility. Knowing what other things can display as unnatural and removing them from the equation will get you that much closer to the truth.

EXAMPLE: Saved by an Angel—Austin, Texas

When working in mental health, I was called to a disturbance where a woman was threatening to kill her three-month-old baby. As I was responding, the woman was holding the child by one leg over the railing of her third story apartment balcony. Patrol officers were on scene trying to calm her. She was screaming that "the devil" was making her, or telling her, to kill the child. Every time the officers would advance to get the child, she would become enraged and swing the infant, threatening to let it go. I was trained as a mediator and was expected to come and fix everything. I am sure the officers really wanted me to hurry and get on scene so they wouldn't be blamed for the catastrophe that was pending.

When I arrived, I came around the backside of the apartment and ascended the open stairwell. There were two officers below the balcony to catch the child, two in the sliding glass door ready to rush in and grab the woman and child, and one at the top of the stairs trying to talk with her. The stairs at the third-floor landing were separated from her balcony by roughly six inches. As I came to the third floor, she saw me. Immediately, she stopped screaming and stared. She brought the baby into her chest and held it there, never blinking her eyes; our eyes remained locked together. She walked toward the side of the balcony, next to the stairs, and I met her there. She handed me the baby. I turned and gave it to the uniformed officer who was previously talking with her. I just went with the flow and raised myself up over the railing and let myself down onto the balcony decking next to her. She reached out and hugged me and began to sob; I hugged her back. I walked her back through her apartment, around the officers, down the stairs to my car and put her in the back; we never spoke. I turned and saw three patrolmen with their mouths open, watching me in confusion. I asked them, "Do you guys need anything else?" As they shook their heads, I got in my car and headed to the hospital. It was that easy.

Two months later, I saw the woman again at the Crisis Unit. She recognized me and said to the psychologist on duty, "That's him! That's the one! He was an angel!" She came over and thanked me. She described her psychological diagnosis along with her postpartum condition and said when she saw me, I was shining white and had a huge halo; I was an angel. That is why she gave the baby up and went with me. She said she was going to kill herself until she saw my aura, and knew God had a plan.

Some people would say this is the hallucination of a schizophrenic, some would say it was postpartum delusions brought on by depression, others would say it was the way the sun reflected off my light-colored hair (back then) and white shirt, and some would attribute it to the early stage cataracts she was developing as a side effect of her multiple medications. This event also could have been entirely paranormal, at least for the woman. Who's to say?

Many years later, author and paranormal consultant Fiona Broome and I were talking one evening, and I told her I have been to many reportedly haunted locations and have never had an experience. She told me she wouldn't have expected so, due to my aura. She stated my aura is very bright and that it would dispel any entities near.

Once again, a case that will go unsolved. The point of this story is, during an interview, you must ask personal medical questions to determine if there is an explainable cause to their experience: drugs, mental illness, or physical impairment. You must ask, no matter what the answer will be. Otherwise, investigators will evaluate your process and say you didn't ask enough questions or the right questions. Witness misinterpretations abound. Be diligent and isolate the possible natural causes before you move on to the paranormal. In doing so, you will be better prepared to detach the people from the actual event.

CHAPTER 9

People and Information

When interviewing people, understand that everyone will tell the story differently. Whether from a different perspective, different levels of assigned importance, or with differing memories of the event, the accounts will not be the same. This can be caused by their relationship to the event, whether they are an eyewitness or repeating the incident from hearsay. Differences could result from an individual's visual or auditory perception problems. Strong influence comes from the folklore, religious, or cultural background of an individual. Many things will influence the information you receive, and many things will influence the interpretation you make out of that information.

The Simplest Explanation

Continuously ensure you are conducting a process of elimination prior to dedicating the time and resources to a project. In doing so, you should always assume there is a perfectly ordinary explanation for the occurrence you are investigating. After all, who has ever heard of an old building having electrical wiring or plumbing problems? Never, right? By approaching the investigation from this perspective and eliminating the simplest of solutions, you will be better able to analyze and isolate the phenomenon. By conducting your investigation in this way, the truly extraordinary will clearly reveal itself.

The study of psychology tells us that misinterpretations by experiencers can be a result of many things. Some observations can be the result of what

I refer to as trigger-memories imbedded in the primal mind. These are the combination of distortions in visual perception, cultural expectations, and personal beliefs. All of this and more can cause these trigger-memories, rooted deep within the subconscious, to activate a fight-or-flight response. During this fight-or-flight, the gaps in the information visually perceived will be filled in with validating information generated from primal or past social or cultural experiences. This can lead to misinterpretations of the event.

Primal Mind

Stress has a unique effect on the human mind. Humans all have, at the core of their consciousness, a reptilian brain structure that contains all our basic drives, such as the need for food, shelter, and procreation; it is the primal brain. Built on top of this foundation are the uniquely human structures providing language, the creative process, logic, and self-awareness. The human side is relatively easy to train, the primal side is very difficult to train, and is, unfortunately, the part of our brain we use most when under increasing stress. That is why when you are calm you can easily get your keys out of your pocket, slide the correct one into the door lock, and open the door.

Under anxiety, or with the threat of violence or fear of assault, completing such a simple task can be overwhelming. Threats or fears of the unknown often cause our brains to revert to primal brain operation, a place devoid of complex language, problem-solving, and fine motor skills. It would be similar to a computer switching over to only operating in its RAM capacity and not having the ability to access its hard drive. When stress is introduced, a fight-or-flight response is activated and the brain switches channels to primal mode. There, we access primal symbols of ancient threats that we are programmed to be wary of; you see a garden hose or crooked stick out of the corner of your eye, subconsciously primal brain kicks in, and you jump to avoid the snake that does not exist. These encoded symbols are often infused in our rationalization of a stressful experience. In this, humans, as well as many other mammals, have an inherent fear of the dark, confinement, heights, and loud noises. This realization may lead to an explanation of why most ghost hunting is primarily conducted at night, or at the very least, in the dark. Or is it the darkness, nighttime, or the hour of the day that falls after sunset that facilitates the exposure of the paranormal experience or opens a door for those conscious enough to see? In any of these cases, it would be irresponsible for an investigator to ignore the human condition response to stress stimuli.

Visual Perception

I have the unique insight of having a certified paraoptometric in my sphere of influence, my wife. She looks into people's eyes every day and can explain the differences in eye structure affecting perception and the many different abnormal conditions that influence the interpretation of what one sees. Recent medical advancements ranging from radial keratotomy (RK) eye surgery to laser-assisted in situ keratomileusis (LASIK) laser surgery have added a whole host of vision side effects and should be noted when interviewing a witness. As an example, these are just four of many medical questions a detective should ask a person who has seen orbs in their house:

Q: Have you had eye surgery or history of an eye injury?
Q: Have you been to an eye doctor recently?
Q: Have you been diagnosed with epilepsy?
Q: Have you ever suffered from ophthalmic migraines (light flashes)?

All these physical conditions, and others, can lead to someone seeing visual phenomena caused by their physical disorder. The argument, in this case, would be whether the physical condition is causing visual perception problems or if the physical condition is allowing your mind to observe and accept the paranormal phenomena that is usually missed or ignored in a normal eye. When addressing these concerns with your witness, be cautious to avoid insulting them due to any perceived physical disability. Just because they may have a visual abnormality does not mean they have not experienced something paranormal.

Cultural Influences

Investigators must not exclude the fact that in all societies and cultures, people pass down passionate beliefs that help explain their world to them.

In the case of a husband massacring his family, is it easier to believe that your most trusted family member could do that, or that a virus or spirit overcomes the loving family member and uses his body to commit murder? The latter would explain how in becoming a werewolf, a man would kill those he loves, wake up in the morning bathed in their blood, and say he didn't do it. It was the monster. It was the curse. Before the scientific method, before the study of psychology and the understanding of blood chemistry, such things fell in line with ancient beliefs. After all, no one could believe a father could do such a thing. Such strongly held beliefs themselves may lead to creating the manifestation of the unexplained. Such beliefs can be concrete in the minds of others and ultimately impossible to prove.

Cultural influences are still strong in our society. Avoiding talking about wrecking your car, because some believe, if you talk about it, somehow it will happen. Assumptions such as these and many others need to be understood by the investigator to make a better-informed decision about the validity of a person's information.

Personal Influence

I remember watching a TV program when I was a kid. It might have been *The Twilight Zone*, or *One Step Beyond*—something like that. The story was about a woman, let's say her name was Anne, who was attacked by a man, and how the stress of the horrific experience landed her in a mental institution. Her husband, let's say his name was Jim, was very angry that this happened but supported her recovery. The day she was released from the hospital, Jim came to pick her up in his car and take her home. They were both happy and heading back to their house when Anne looked out the car window and pointed. "That's him! That's the man!" Well, subsequently, Jim was filled with overwhelming rage. He pulled over, got out, killed the man with his bare hands, and then hid the body. He jumped back into the car, worried about what he'd done but satisfied that he vindicated his wife and sped away. They drove another couple blocks and Anne pointed. "No... that's the man...That's him!"

Our personal experiences dictate our expectation of an event, and those memories from our interpretation of that event. Depending on our emotional background histories, each person can uniquely and differently describe an experience shared by two individuals.

Understanding your experiencer's background is an important facet of the investigation. Being mindful of important experiences in their lives and their reactions to them gives a clearer picture for the investigator to assess. This approach will help guide you to the type of interview you should conduct.

Chapter 10
Types of Interviews

There are many different types of interviews and many different companies making money teaching these interview techniques. The Reid Technique is one of the most famous. While conceptually it is an in-depth study of human behavior and responses, it also can be condensed to just a handful of steps. And that is the way of most types of interviews. Most practiced interviewers strive to incorporate the many different portions of the various techniques into their own interview style. Witnesses can see through a person who is typically not empathetic to their situation, instead simply trying to mimic a compassionate interview position. You need to be your own interviewer, with your own voice and style; just don't miss anything.

What to Ask

The questions to ask should be in tune with your mindset of the investigation. It is rare for law enforcement officers to initiate an interview already knowing everything in an attempt to acquire a confession. While interviewers should prepare extensively before they conduct an interview, most times your information is very limited. Using deductive reasoning, you as the investigator should formulate the possibilities of what happened and go from there.

In a paranormal investigation, you may have little or no information before you go into an interview. You may have just the understanding that a person knows of a haunting and you meet to hear their story. In many cases, in the beginning of an investigation, you may not even know what you should be asking. Initially, the best thing to do is follow basic interview techniques, develop your instincts, and conduct a lot of interviews to become practiced.

In the course of questioning a person, ask open-ended questions that cannot be answered with a yes or no. Avoid leading questions that will point the person toward providing information in your favor.

Question examples:

Ask this: "What do you remember most about this house?"
Not this: "Did you see the blood stains on the floor of the house?"

Ask this: "Did you hear any noise outside the house?"
Not this: "Did you hear the car drive by the house?"

When you ask leading questions, it is an indication that you are not experienced in your craft, or that you are intentionally grooming or leading the person being interviewed to support your ghost hunt. If you are inexperienced, that is okay, learn from your mistakes and move on. We cannot get better at what we do if we do not point out what we do wrong and then take measures to correct it.

The Standard or Basic Interview

It is through witnesses and eyewitnesses (the experiencer) that the investigator obtains most of his information, and it is through that information that he formulates additional questions. The basic interview consists of:

Who?
What?
When?
Where?
Why?
How?

These are the skeletal structures of the body of the event. Without answering these simple foundation questions, your investigative monster cannot stand. In many initial paranormal events, these questions are unknown to the experiencer. They can answer the questions unique to themselves of what happened to them, when, where, and how, but the who did it and why it occurred are usually the most difficult to narrow down. That is where the benefit of historical research comes in. If you cover these 5 Ws, you will have a good beginning to your paranormal quest. Once these questions are answered, you will have a working foundation to explore their senses.

After the basic interview of who, what, when, where, and why—and before attempting to explore the environmental and personal experiences in a memory retrieval cognitive interview (this does not always happen in a sequential way)—I will often readdress the events and focus on what the person's senses picked up during the event:

Sight
Smell
Hearing
Taste
Touch

The senses often awaken additional memories about the event. Let's say that during the basic interview, the experiencer tells you they saw a shadow figure in their doorway, and that was the main focus of their story. After allowing them to go all the way through the experience uninterrupted, you take them back to the beginning. This time, you focus on the specific event, in this case the shadow figure. You no longer ask about what they saw, you ask about what they heard, if anything, in the background; a dog barking, a siren in the distance, the wind blowing, anything else unrelated to the phenomenon. Then you ask what the atmosphere felt like, what their skin felt like during the event. What did they smell, was there a taste in their mouth (metallic), and so on. These senses will be recorded in their mind subconsciously and need to be brought forward through active questions about them; otherwise, the person being interviewed will most likely overlook these feelings as unimportant.

In some cases, paranormal witnesses will repeat what they have heard others say, such as, "One time, I was at the Yegua (yeah-wah) County Store in Lee County, Texas and this old man said he saw a ghost lantern down by the creek. Supposedly it was a lantern from a Confederate soldier that was looking for the treasure he had buried in the area." These types of repeated stories may be factual; however, because the person who experienced the event is not the one telling them, it is considered hearsay. While hearsay is not admissible in court, it can be valuable in paranormal investigations and should not be discounted. Hearsay might be supported by other interviews later. Make sure you discuss all hearsay information provided to you.

Concluding the Interview

So often, we as the investigators believe we know how to conduct an investigation. However, the witness or experiencer may have some insights that will help. When you complete your interview, make sure you ask them a few additional questions when appropriate:

1. Is there anything that you haven't told me that you think might be important to the investigation?
2. What do you think is causing this?
3. What steps would you take?
4. Who would you talk to?
5. Where would you go?

Many times, I have interviewed witnesses and suspects and later found they withheld crucial information. When asked why, the usual response was, "You didn't ask." After conducting a standard interview and concluding with the above final questions, you should have enough information to begin an extensive research campaign to validate what they have told you so far. Assuming they are being truthful.

The Cognitive Interview

In the early 1900s, Hugo Munsterberg, a Harvard professor, conducted a study in an attempt to identify and isolate memory retrieval techniques to be used for witnesses. He was working on his earlier premise that eyewitness testimony was remarkably faulty; however, it could be improved through specific questioning techniques. His work was largely ignored by law enforcement and court officials. Later, in the 1970s, his premise was revisited, and ultimately R. Edward Geiselman and others came up with what was later coined the Cognitive Interview. I have found that using the Cognitive Interview technique after a Standard Interview always gets more information for the investigation. While the Cognitive Interview technique is typically in the form of a written witness statement, I usually ask them the questions and rarely have them write their experiences down.

The Cognitive Interview consists of four basic steps:

1. During the interview, try to isolate the interviewee's mind within the location of the event. Describe it by eliminating everything around it. Tell them to think only of this place and describe it in detail. Ask them to describe their feelings at the time of the event. Have them describe their reactions to the event.
2. Tell the interviewee that some people hold back information because they are not sure of exactly what they remember. Tell them not to edit anything out, even if they think it is not significant.
3. After allowing the witness to tell their story in their own way, have them tell the story in the reverse order of the events. Also, the interviewer can pick a specific time in the story that is important and have the witness go from there, proceeding both forward and backward.
4. Lastly, have the witness adopt the perspective of others who were present and have them speculate on what the others may have seen.

Research has revealed that both cognitive and hypnosis procedures elicit a significantly greater number of correct items of information from the witness than a Standard Interview.

Memory-Event Similarity Interview

Experiential (Experience) memory tends to be emotional memory, something more than just memorization. Memory-event similarity is a technique in which the interviewer possesses the knowledge of the environment the witness experienced during the event because of the previous information gathered in the Standard and Cognitive Interviews. Therefore, the interviewer has the event knowledge and then describes the environment to the witness to reinstate, in the witness's mind, the external influences they earlier described. This would be the weather, unusual sounds, the time of day, emotions such as fear or happiness, and cognitive thoughts such as they need to open the door, turn on the light, or run. The interviewer takes them back by restating what the witnesses previously explained, walking them step-by-step back through the environment: "It was completely dark"—wait for the witness's response; "the air was completely still"—wait for the witness's response; "you hear the train in the distance"—wait for the witness's response; "it smelled stale, musty." And so on. This technique will also help clarify information by having the interviewer describe his understanding of the scene and the witness correcting anything that is not true.

Witness-Attuned Questioning

Interviewers who can imagine themselves in the witness's place can more readily ask pertinent questions. By placing himself or herself in the witness's frame of mind, the interviewer can project onto the witness questions the witnesses should have been asking themselves. The interviewer may say, "If I were you, I would wonder if someone were trying to scare me." Or, "What does the apparition want?" Or, "If this happened to me, I would wonder if I were dreaming." These types of questions will open further dialogue with the witness and often lead to more answers about the event.

Use of Hypnosis

The use of hypnosis in law enforcement is considered controversial, but it can be used as another interviewing tool, just like a polygraph. As with a lie detector, suspects in a criminal episode can have legitimate reasons not to participate. It is rare in criminal cases that participating in a hypnosis or a polygraph examination will help out the suspect. However, while investigating the paranormal, hypnosis may help unlock repressed memories of someone who has experienced a particularly stressful or terrifying event. When induced into a hypnotic state, the person may be better able to remember specific things about the event or people and things within the event.

If a paranormal team elects to use hypnosis, it would be advised to follow an industry standard practice. Law enforcement has the most demanding standards set by State v. Hurd. In that case, six rules were endorsed to be followed:

1. A licensed psychiatrist or psychologist must conduct hypnosis.
2. The person performing the hypnosis should be independent of the investigation.
3. All questions will be kept as a record in written format.
4. A pre-interview must be conducted to keep the original information separate from the information gleaned from the hypnosis interview.
5. The session should be videotaped.
6. Only the hypnotist and subject should be present at the session.

So, the question is, how many psychiatrists or psychologists who perform hypnosis will volunteer to do this? If they agree, most will not do it for free. It is my belief that if a person becomes a certified hypnotist from an accredited agency, that should suffice for the needs of a paranormal investigation. I know cops who are certified in hypnosis interviews who do a great job. There is no reason a paranormal investigator could not obtain a certification and do the same with the voluntary consent of the witness.

Effective Testimony
There is often a debate about what effective testimony is. Is it a well-rehearsed story, told convincingly in a concise and chronological manner? Is it a passionately told tale filled with emotional range and conviction? Is it a scattered testimonial of bits and pieces of fact and assumption? Whatever

it is, many people view it differently and interpret the story in the way they relate to the world. I have faced situations in law enforcement where citizens mistrusted me and did not believe anything I told them, even though I was absolutely telling the truth. I am sure that most people reading this book have had some sort of similar experience with a co-worker, friend, or loved one. No matter the truth, they were not going to believe what you told them. This is why understanding effective testimony is so important.

Effective testimony is a combination of how the information is delivered, by whom, and how it is received. As a paranormal investigator, you must take in the information and be able to sort the wheat from the chaff, the important from the unimportant. Effective testimony of a physical phenomenon will be interpreted differently in an audience full of physics students, or an audience of religious scholars, or an audience of ufologists. Effective testimony is testimony that presents the facts in plain language with no jargon and is comprehensible to the layperson. Cool catch phrases and acronyms do not indicate a higher level of credibility or competency. Effective testimony is about getting the information understood.

CHAPTER 11

Overcoming Interview Challenges

Please do not misunderstand the intent of this chapter. But here is a simple fact: the paranormal field is fraught with intentional deception. Everything from haunted restaurant and bar marketing to event staging. It is your responsibility as a fact finder to establish the differences between those who are just having fun and those who are set up to deceive.

In most investigations, the persons involved are relatively cooperative. Depending on the severity of the crime, the depth of their involvement, and the length of their required participation, their attitude toward the case will adjust accordingly. A witness in a murder case may feel a strong obligation to give testimony, where the same person may not want to get involved in a simple theft because they feel their time is valuable and not worth pursuing a trivial matter.

On the other hand, a person's involvement can become more complex, and often, you come to realize the witness is more involved than you first thought.

Dealing with Hostile Witnesses

It's not uncommon for friends and family members of the suspect to be considered hostile witnesses. A hostile witness can be someone who has a vested interest in getting the suspect's charges dropped or just simply does not want to participate. In paranormal investigations, hostile witnesses are usually the debunkers and doubters surrounding an event. They may see the spirit of their grandmother right in front of them and will flatly refuse to believe it was anything other than a natural occurrence. Sometimes these can be people within the paranormal field itself. I have seen ufologists laugh at ghost hunters, cryptozoologists make fun of spiritualists, and demonologists disparage psychics; sometimes we are our own worst enemies. Bottom line, if you cannot prove the other person's experience does not exist, keep an open mind. The work they are doing may one day support your hypothesis.

It is rare to have a productive dialogue with a hostile witness. If they are someone who is open to questioning, by all means, get as much information as possible. If they are not, leave them alone and move on. Spend your energy on something productive.

Cross Examination vs. Interrogation of the Hoaxer

It was reported that P.T. Barnum said, "There is a sucker born every minute." However, this was most likely not an original quote from Barnum since the phrase was used in an article in *European Magazine* in 1806, four years before Barnum was born. This fact is another example that we are suckers and believe much of what we hear—me included. In dealing with a hoaxer, one needs to determine their motive. Is it for fun, harm, or profit? And so you ask, what is the difference between interviewing and interrogating? That is simple: the person under interrogation must be aware they are being accused of something. In an interview, you are simply gathering information. In an interviewer's cross-examination, the interviewer is merely confirming what the witness said and confirming the validity of their testimony, unlike court cross-examination, which is to try to put holes in the other's testimony.

When a paranormal investigator uses cross-examination, they are going over areas of the story that are inconsistent in order to better understand the elements of the event. In the paranormal field, if you choose to interrogate someone, you must be mindful about the raised eyebrow or shaking of the head, unintentional motions or a statement that discredits the witness's account directly. What course you use is something you will have to decide for yourself. It is a judgment call.

Dealing with hoaxers in the paranormal field is as precarious as dealing with liars in criminal cases. The question is, do you let them know you know they are lying? By calling them out, will it help you or the paranormal field, or injure it? Will it serve a positive purpose or create havoc? Whether it is the right thing to do or not, sometimes doing the right thing is detrimental. Sometimes, letting a reported fictional ghost event go is the right course of action. However, if what the hoaxer is saying or doing is intended to harm or defraud someone, it is the responsibility of the paranormal community to expose them.

So, if you choose to interrogate the hoaxer, it is because you have affirmative physical evidence of their deception. Preparation is everything. You must have absolute proof that the event could not have happened the way the hoaxer described it or have physical evidence that they staged it. Most people do not react well to being called a liar so be aware of their reaction: anger, ambivalence, passion, or defeat. Each of these emotions can mean the person is lying or the person is telling the truth; you must examine the totality of the person, their story, and their motives to determine truth or lie. Ask yourself, does it make sense for them to lie to you?

In the interrogation, you need not only to know a lot about the event but also to have a good understanding about the person's history and personality. Just because someone looks up and to the right does not mean they are lying. If you choose the interrogation, understand that, unlike law enforcement, the person does not have to put up with it. They can leave. Once they leave, all their information is gone. Before you burn that bridge, make sure you get as much out of them as you can, before you accuse them of being a hoaxer.

The Interrogation Setting
There have been many examples of people that for either personal manipulation or profit, intentionally report an incident, or set up a false paranormal event. If you discover this you can either (1) leave it alone and go on, (2) speak secretly about the fraud with your friends, (3) out them in public and social media, or (4) talk with them privately and guide them to accepting what you know as true.

If you are comfortable with the person and decide to speak with them, you may elect to choose a setting that is private, where you can address them with your accusation. If they are a reasonable person, they will feel more comfortable about admitting to their dishonesty in such a setting. This would give them the opportunity to apologize and go on their way without further drama. If you feel they will be hostile, you may elect to have others in the room with you or address your accusation in a public place, in the hopes the person will not act out. In any case, dealing with a hoaxer is uncomfortable business, and I wish you the best.

Interviews and Statement Examinations

In this book, I talk a lot about interviewing because I feel it is the most important part of the investigation. It is the thing that will discriminate the mentally ill from the truly gifted, the misunderstood from the hoaxer, and the innocent from a malicious opportunist. As an honest investigator, you will spend a lot of time talking with people about the incident. Some will be forthcoming; others will have to be coaxed. Some will relay vivid recall of their memory, and others will have to be regressed to the time they experienced the event. Others will deliberately mislead you for any number of reasons. You will need to have the ability to take it all in, identify the information that fits, then isolate the common core facts. You are looking for consistency in their stories—events and facts that relate positively to one another.

Related Truths

The common or core facts are the main identifying elements of the event. When interviewing witnesses, it is important to keep track of the core facts of the described incident. It is the correlation of core facts that will provide a roadmap to your destination, which is finding out the truth. In many cases, the person you are interviewing is retelling a story they have heard or relaying something that they believe to be true because they know it to be a part of the community lore, stemming from a credible source.

Identifying the common facts of the story allows the investigator to create a concise and chronological report of the event: (1) a beginning that usually starts with a ghost story, (2) a middle, which consists of the investigation, and (3) an end where the investigator concludes their findings and makes a determination of what happened. All three parts must be present. In some cases, one person might know only one or two of these common facts. When this happens, the goal should be to interview several people in order to gather enough information to complete the story.

When dealing with violations of the law, people will often omit key elements of the common or core facts. It is your job, as the person collecting the information, to identify these omissions and try to isolate the reason for such exclusions. Sometimes, when a person tells a story, they embellish in order to emphasize a key element, emotion, or person. For the same reason, people telling a story may diminish certain elements, emotions, or persons relayed in the event. Either one of these diversions can be isolated and identified if you pay attention to the storyteller's normal speech patterns, the complexity in which they tell the story (step-by-step chronological order), and any deviations from these.

As an example, I have responded to several deceased persons cases in which the wife of the deceased told me of (1) the before events of death, such as exercising, (2) the during events, such as falling down and not breathing, and (3) the after events, such as waiting for emergency assistance to arrive. She may neglect to say that after death they moved the body and put his underwear back on, or that they wiped his mouth with a tissue to remove lipstick transferred during the CPR process, or from other activities. When honest persons intentionally deviate, they do it from a survival instinct and do not mean to cause harm to the investigation. This behavior often makes them appear to be untrustworthy, when in fact they just need to gain your trust in order to be completely truthful.

Vetting the Witness

Most people are surprised to learn that a reported witness to an event was not a witness to the event. They were not on the same street, in the same town, or even visiting the same state where the report occurred. It is amazing how many people will try to include themselves in an event when they had nothing to do with the occurrence. Everything from the benign ghost sighting to stolen valor to admittance in committing a sensational crime, some people feel the need for recognition. Many of these people mean no real harm by telling a little white lie about seeing the specter of their grandma overlooking their children, or about the local legend of the railroad track ghost children, or Crybaby Bridge. It is those who inflate the story and add themselves as an eyewitness who damage the paranormal research and confuse the true search for answers. At some point in every long-spun ghost tale, the truth of the event can become so uncertain that no real conclusion of when, where, and why the event occurred, may ever come about. Therefore, vetting the witness is so important.

When I worked the streets on patrol, one of my closest partners was an Eagle Scout as a kid. He and two other fellow Eagle Scouts told me several stories about their experiences. Now, some Eagle Scouts are known for their uncompromising character and ingenuity, but some are not. They all told me several stories that happened to them and their groups when they would go off to camp in the summer. How strange events occurred, sounds pierced the night, lights flickered in the forest, and other oddities heightened their awareness and imagination. They told me how some of the scoutmasters would tell them about the escaped mental patient or prison convict who was supposedly seen in the area, or the wolf or mountain lion, and how someone near had been attacked. They even had tales of the scoutmasters or friends of the scoutmasters dressing up in costume and scaring the kids. In such situations, it is easy to create the next man-eating wolf tale or Blackjack Monster legend. And, it is because of stories such as these that skepticism is healthy.

Any good investigator, in any investigative field, will first look to where the money goes; most crimes circle around this very thing. Follow the money. This can also be traced in the world of the paranormal. When considering a witness, you must examine their motivations. Who stands to gain the most from promoting a reported paranormal event? Whether it is a criminal or paranormal investigation, it is important that you as an investigator identify the motive of the event or reported event.

The Motives

Essentially, there are three types of motives attributed to a witness. One is a simple or universal motive, another is a particularized motive, and the last is an unspecified motive. Each can add or subtract from the credibility of the witness. I have adapted the motives for the paranormal as simple, specified, and unspecified:

Simple motive. This applies to anyone wanting to report a paranormal event as well as to those in authority wanting to validate what they experienced. There appears to be no other reason to report the event other than curiosity about the nature and meaning of the event.

Specified motive. The specified motive should always raise a caution flag because it is usually generated by owners of properties who want to advertise them as haunted attractions. They are not interested in cleaning the location or removing some malevolent reputation; on the contrary, they are looking for a marketing opportunity. Other people may want their business or home to be known as haunted and may be seeking attention, recognition, or pity. Whatever the reason, when you interview someone who wants a haunting, be especially skeptical.

Unspecified motive. In some cases, those persons suffering from mental illness or a mental condition may perceive a haunting, possession, or other event that is entirely created from a delusional mind. These conditions can result in visual and auditory hallucinations. However, do not discount the events described by persons with these conditions. Just because someone is mentally imbalanced does not mean that what they see, hear, or feel is not happening. Just be aware of events that cannot be true.

So, as I have hinted throughout this book, skepticism, not cynicism, is the key to unlocking the truth of the investigation. There are two main parts of any paranormal investigation: (1) researching the history of the event, and (2) gathering evidence to support the event. Once you have obtained convincing reviewable research with credible vetted witnesses and gathered unmolested evidence attributed to the phenomena, you may have a true, sustainable, and founded paranormal event.

CHAPTER 12
The Stories We Tell

Anytime you use people as your single source of information, you are setting yourself up for inconsistencies from your source and criticism from your peers. I spoke at length with Aron Houdini, the master escape artist, about this very dilemma. He had been involved in several paranormal cases where both the investigators and witnesses provided less than credible information and owners of reported haunted locations were attempting to capitalize from it. In a particular case, the owner of the property actually installed hidden speakers in the wall to create creaks, bumps, and other suspicious noises. When asked about this, the owner said they only used it for when they did a Halloween haunted house to scare the tourists. Don't get me wrong, if you want to have a Halloween haunted house business, that's fine, but combining hoaxes where an investigator expect facts is not a good idea.

When faced with knowledge of a hoax, the challenge is how you are going to handle it. Do you confront them on scene? Wait until you can speak with them in private? Talk to them on the phone or send them an email? Or, do you blast out your accusation on social media? The unique situation may be the very thing that dictates your response and the actions you take.

How ever you decide to handle it, be professional—always strive to maintain your credibility.

Misconduct

There is misconduct in every facet of human existence. It is commonplace in the professions of law, health care, politics, and general business. Because of the frequency of misconduct, many people have reservations about buying used cars, working with sales persons, and any other number of things in which there is a desire to obtain the clients' money. This situation is completely understandable. Thankfully, there are regulatory entities that enforce a standard of conduct within most professions. Individuals found violating procedural, ethical, or industry standards should be reported and disciplined through forms of sanctions, fines, or imprisonment, depending on the severity of their offense and their intent. The problem within the paranormal world is the difficulty in proving a phenomenon occurred in the first place. Likewise, it is difficult to prove that it didn't occur—unless it is caused by a person perpetrating a hoax or scam on an unsuspecting consumer.

One such widespread scam was the highly televised Psychic Readers Network where Youree Dell Harris, better known as Miss Cleo from Jamaica, advertised psychic readings priced by the minute. Access Resource Services d/b/a Psychic Readers Network was sued in numerous lawsuits brought by several states. Ultimately, the Federal Trade Commission (FTC) charged the owners of the company with deceptive advertising, billing, and collection practices to the tune of one billion dollars. The case was settled for $500 million. Subsequently, the Psychic Readers Network was shut down. Miss Cleo was never charged with a crime, but the FTC accused her of misleading the public and that she was merely an actress portraying a psychic. Unfortunately, there are many other organizations on TV and through other media sources that prey on people in the same way.

If a person or an organization is intentionally falsely presenting their abilities or creating an atmosphere that would lead people to believe a psychic or paranormal event has occurred, there is an ethical obligation to provide the truth of your facts without adding false information. Those who falsify damage the true paranormal investigative field and stigmatize others who are truly working to discover the root of psychic ability and the causes of paranormal phenomena.

Skepticism not Cynicism

There are many well-documented examples of paranormal fraud. During the United States Spiritualist movement in the mid-1850s, the Fox Sisters reportedly fooled millions of people with their abilities to communicate with the other side. Likewise, some twentieth-century photos of the Loch Ness Monster are very compelling—the most famous of which is the 1934 "surgeon's photo" reportedly taken by Doctor Robert Wilson. The picture has become iconic in the cryptozoology world. It depicts what looks to be the long neck and head of a creature protruding out of the water. A cropped version of the photo was featured on the cover of the *Daily Mail* in 1934. In the 1930s, people merely debated its authenticity. However, with today's technologies the photo can be disproven simply based on the dimensions of the water's wave patterns and the science of fluid dynamics. Also, the cropped version eliminated a view of the shoreline making the cropped version difficult to determine the size of the creature. And then there is Uri Geller, the self-reported, spoon-bending mentalist who caused years of controversy and ultimately recreated himself as an entertainer.

Skepticism is required in all theaters of life. Unfortunately, there are many people who fall into the category of the True Believer Syndrome. This term was popularized by the late fraudulent psychic M. Lamar Keene. Even though he revealed techniques of deception used by him and other reported psychics, many people still continued to believe in psychics and ignored the fact that anyone can appear to be a psychic if he knows the secrets behind the tricks. Please remember, psychics are different than mystics and other religious leaders.

In 1996, former stage magician James Randi created the James Randi Educational Foundation (JREF) to help people defend themselves against paranormal and pseudoscientific fraud. According to the JREF, many psychics employ a technique known as cold reading. They tell the subjects nothing, but make guesses, put out suggestions, and ask questions. Conducting a cold reading can be a deceptive art, and the unwary observer may come away believing that unknown information was developed through some paranormal channels or wondrous means. This is not so if the psychic is specifically employing a cold reading technique. For example, the reader will say, "I get an older man here." This statement is simultaneously a question, a suggestion, and a guess by the reader, who expects some reaction from the person being read or the audience, and usually gets it. That reaction may just be a nod, the actual name of a person, or an identification (brother, husband, grandfather), by the subject, not by the reader. Employing such techniques can indicate there may be a fraud present.

The JREF supports grassroots skeptic groups to help them organize and promote skeptical and critical thinking, and thus help people avoid scams that take advantage of innocent, naïve, and grieving people who are susceptible to the false hope that profits con artists. For years, the JREF has offered a one-million-dollar prize to anyone who can prove a paranormal event or psychic ability. Their rules are stringent, and so far, no one has claimed the million dollars.

Remember, skepticism is usually about adopting an inquisitive position concerning information, evidence, ideas and beliefs. It questions declarations that are taken for granted elsewhere. Skepticism is a healthy attitude that all effective investigators should adopt.

EXAMPLE: Home Sweet Home—Lake Travis, Texas

One evening several years ago, while working uniformed patrol in a rural area of Central Texas, I responded to a family disturbance. The dispatcher reported that a man called 911 and requested the police. There was yelling in the background and then the line went silent. When I arrived, I shut off my car lights and drove down the driveway. This was a huge house, very close to the lake, with a manicured lawn, gorgeous flowerbeds and BMWs in the garage. I met a man and woman at the front door. I knew my backup was only a couple of minutes behind me, so I asked the woman to step out onto the porch and sit on a bench. The front door had a large pane glass window, so I asked the man to stand in the hallway where I could see him, but out of sight from the woman, and I closed the door. They were quiet, polite, and cooperative. Both even smiled at me, a little. With the door closed, they could not hear each other talking. The woman stated they were having marital problems and got into a verbal altercation. She said everything was fine and it just got heated. She confirmed that no one got physical and they both just needed to calm down. She volunteered to leave the house for the night to make sure nothing more happened. I asked her to stay on the bench and went to talk with the man. He confirmed what she had said and also offered to leave for the night. At face value, it seemed like a simple disagreement.

My backup arrived, a training officer and a rookie in the field-training program. I told the rookie, who was going to manage the scene, that I had separated the persons involved while waiting for him to arrive. The rookie promptly pulled out his notepad and identified the woman on the porch, then got her story of the event, which was exactly what she had told me. Then he went to the man and repeated the same. And again, the man told him what he had told me.

While the rookie was doing the interview under the not so watchful eye of the training officer, I checked the kitchen, living room, and bedrooms. In the bedroom, I found a broken chair, and the sheets from the bed were pulled halfway off. Pieces of a smashed cell phone were in the master bathroom. When I returned, I walked in on the rookie telling the man and woman, who were now together standing in the entryway, that one of them could leave for the night, and that would be best. I stopped the rookie and asked him to come outside with me, out of earshot of the couple. I asked the rookie if he had seen anything unusual. The rookie said, "No." I asked if he had looked, and the rookie did not answer. I brought the rookie back to the man and asked to see the man's arms; he had a single fresh scratch on one forearm. I asked him to pull up the legs to his warm-up pants; there were three in-line scratches there.

I took the rookie out to the porch and spoke with the woman about the scratches. Her story changed, and the anger returned. She began yelling about telling him to sleep in the guest bedroom and not in her bed, and how she tried to pull him out of the bed by the legs and grabbed his phone when he made the 911 call. There were two criminal offenses: (1) assault with injury—family violence, and (2) interference with a 911 phone call.

When you are investigating anything, you have to take into consideration the environment, the witnesses' behavior, and their explanation. Does the situation or what they tell you make sense? If the answer is no, you must continue your examination. Skepticism is one of the most important traits any investigator has.

Remember, the scene always changes when you, the investigator, arrive. Individual behavior always changes when the individual knows they are being observed.

In my example, dispatch receives a call from (1) a man asking for help from the police, (2) there is yelling in the background, and (3) the phone abruptly disconnects. You must ask about each event you have knowledge of and determine if the explanation is reasonable. If it is not, or there seems to be more to it, you must dig deeper. In this case, the rookie was blindly conducting a basic interview and believing everything the people involved were saying; always a huge mistake.

The Lies We Tell

Bottom line, people are liars—there's a little liar in all of us. Some of the most common places we lie are in relationships, with family and friends, work associates, and through community endeavors. Leonard Saxe, Ph.D., a polygraph expert and professor of psychology at Brandeis University, said in a 2016 *Psychology Today* article, "Lying has long been a part of everyday life. We couldn't get through the day without being deceptive."

Studies have shown that in a 10-minute conversation between two strangers, people will tell at least one lie. If self-esteem is in question, the rate of lies increases dramatically. In England, men average six lies a day and women only three. Many times, these lies are nothing more than to make the conversation more interesting or to cover up personal feelings or failures: "There's nothing's wrong, I am fine." "No, those pants don't make your butt look big." "I had no cell signal." "The traffic was terrible." "It was on sale." "I have a headache." Or, as the Blues Brothers' Joliet Jake would say: "I ran out of gas. I didn't have enough money for cab fare. My tux didn't come back from the cleaners. There was an earthquake, a terrible flood, locusts! It wasn't my fault!" Deception in everyday life is part of human culture and part of our social structure. That is why it is so difficult to detect. Doctor Saxe goes on to say that even though we are socialized and should always tell the truth, society often encourages and even rewards deception. If you show up late for work, Saxe explains, when you say you overslept you will receive far more punishment than if you were to lie and say you were stuck in traffic.

Unlike law enforcement, in the paranormal field, a person does not feel they have to lie to stay out of jail; they merely have to lie to continue their hoax, or, ironically, they will continue to lie to not look like a liar. It is a credibility issue on the part of the hoaxer; if they change their story, they will look like fakes, and they do not want that.

Remember, skepticism and cynicism are two different things. Skepticism is what helps move the investigation forward. Cynicism closes all doors to the possibilities.

Signals of Deception

It always helps to know how a person normally acts and then contrast their normal behavior with deception indicators, but that is not usually the situation for an investigator. So, in turn, investigators should be aware of certain signals that could indicate deception. These signals may or may not actually mean someone is trying to be deceptive; however, they are additional cues you should be aware of that could save you valuable investigative time. These indicators involve body language, facial expressions, and speech patterns. The following are not necessarily, but can be, indications of deception. The more indicators you cue in on, the more likely the person is lying:

Flushing of the skin. In cases with people who are fair-skinned, flushing can be seen under stress, and intentional deception can cause this.

Increase in breathing. Increased breathing is a fight-or-flight response and can be caused because subconsciously, this person wants to run away, and their body is preparing them to do so.

Rapid head tilt. The person may jerk their head to the side, bow lightly, or jerk back, in response to what they want you to think is a shocking and ridiculous question.

Rigid body posture. Many times, people who prepare themselves for an interview know their body movements will be analyzed. Therefore, they over correct and try not to move at all.

Repeating words they have said. Repeating words buys them time to analyze the question and formulate the lie. This is a true giveaway. Question:

Where were you this afternoon? Answer: "Where was I?" Deception... deception...deception.

Providing too much information. Many times, people stray from the conversation, and that is natural. However, to change topics or veer attention to an entirely other event is a sign of deception.

Touching or covering the mouth. When the finger goes up to the lips/mouth and they say something like, "Let's see, where was I? Yeah, I was at my brother's house," it is deceptive behavior.

Covering vulnerable parts of the body. This is another fight-or-flight response. Subconsciously they will cover parts of their body vulnerable to assault: head, face, and sexual organs.

Shuffling the feet. Besides those with restless leg syndrome, this person wants to run away from you so badly they cannot keep their feet still.

Mouth becomes dry and it is difficult for them to speak. This is also a stress response from fight-or-flight. Salivary glands slow down because it's not time to eat; it's time to fight.

Using fingers to point out or at things. This comes from frustration and anger. In their attempt to get out of their deception they will try to blame the interviewer or distract the questioning to another person or event.

Maintaining unnatural eye contact. Overcompensating for deceptive eye movement will cause liars to try to eliminate eye movement altogether.

Making certain eye movements. This is a controversial subject, and in my opinion, by itself it means very little, but here we go. As you are facing the person, these eye movements could indicate the following:

> Up and to the Left – They are searching for an image to construct.
> Up and to the Right – They are looking for an image in memory.
> To the Left – They are searching for a sound to construct.
> To the Right – They are looking for a sound in memory.
> Down and to the Left – They are looking for a feeling, smell, or taste in memory.
> Down and to the Right – Usually caused by internal dialogue and they talk to themselves.

However, when retrieving memories, studies say a person makes about one eye movement per second. When there is no eye movement, it indicates the person has rehearsed what they are going to say many times and do not have to search for what they are going to say. This too indicates deception.

So, it is reasonable to say that an investigator should not rely on a single deception detection method. Each can be a cue, and the more cues, the more likely they are being deceptive.

Dealing with Paranormal Fraud

In the case of possible paranormal fraud, action must be taken; it is your duty to do so. There are different kinds of fraud:

Staging false phenomena. Manipulators use methods of gathering information by asking certain questions to make it seem that they know more about the person through psychic intelligence, or they have a mechanism to find out information about their client before they do a reading. Proprietors of reportedly haunted sites could set up speakers or covert lights in order to fake ghost apparitions. The real question is—what is the mental state of the person who does this? In law enforcement it is referred to as culpable mental states: (1) intentional, (2) knowing, (3) reckless, or (4) criminal negligence.

Intentional fraud. This is the most egregious form of paranormal fraud. A person intentionally creates a false paranormal environment to prey on a vulnerable person for monetary gain.

Examples are hoaxed UFO experiences, false hauntings, faked séances, and fallacious card readings.

Perpetuating a fraud. Having the knowledge of paranormal fraud and taking actions to perpetuate it.

An example is a person continuing to promote a location as legitimately haunted when they have knowledge to the contrary, i.e., the moaning sounds are made from an underground gas line.

Reckless fraud. Creating a situation for fun and not dismissing the event after the actions are taken and the people exposed continue to think the event was real.

An example is teenagers pouring grain alcohol onto a tombstone and lighting it on fire when their friends walk through the cemetery at night.

Negligent fraud. Having the knowledge that an event is false but not taking any measures to expose it.

An example is witnessing a person manipulate equipment to cause an effect.

Do not misunderstand the intent of these four mental states. They are a challenge to exposing fraud, not some accusatory gesture to those setting up "haunted houses" for fun and profit. These mental states pertain specifically to those persons attempting to defraud others by falsifying paranormal events, thus harming others by making them believe in such events.

Exception to the Rule Rules?
If you or your ghost-hunting group want to head out into the dark woods, drink beer, and look for the Blair Witch, so be it. That's fun; I've been there. The legitimacy problem comes when you or your group try to mesh the two together. If a location is supposed to be a legitimate place of paranormal activity, treat it as such. Pulling out your whoopee-cushion when there is a serious investigation in progress dilutes everyone's credibility.

PART THREE
The Research

CHAPTER 13
Getting to the Facts

I know, sitting down in a library or an old, dusty courthouse reading piles of faded paper records, microfiche slides, or ancient newspapers is the least sexy part of a paranormal investigation, yet usually the most rewarding. I actually like it. In my regular job as a detective, I may discover one or two clues in a day. But from the documents at the Austin Historical Society, I can discover dozens of tangible bits of information in just an hour.

When dealing with research, you soon understand that time causes the verbal explanation of an occurrence to change into an anecdote. The anecdote then alters into tale, and the tale transforms into legend. It is through the constant reinterpretation of the original occurrence by human storytelling and information passing that dilutes its reality. Thankfully, physical records and photographs are not affected by the human memory or its limitless creativity.

Loose Associations

If you are lucky enough to be the first person to get the details on an event, information gathering is easy. A conversation starts, it leads to a paranormal topic, and the witness segues into their ghost story. That's how it usually happens. While it might be entertaining, the storyteller typically has little specific knowledge of the original event, the names of the persons involved, or the persons who witnessed the occurrence.

This is where your value as a researcher comes in. You should know where to look for documented information about records related to the event, and you should establish if there are any living persons who can answer questions about it. Somewhere in there, you have to make a determination if it is truth or an urban legend.

Urban legends are why many of us have paranormal interests. While they are usually based on hearsay and widely circulated, some of their origins are true. One of the most popular is the 1930s tale about the Florida alligator taken to New York City as a pet and subsequently let loose or flushed into the sewer system where he, she, or they thrived and became enormous beasts killing and eating the homeless that wandered into the tunnels seeking shelter—how disturbing is that?

Alas, this story has been investigated. No substantial evidence has ever been recovered, nor have any bodies ever been found with wounds appearing to be related to alligator bites. Yet, the stories and sightings still abound in the primary and secondary schools of the city. This legend continues because there is the possibility that live alligators were released into the New York city sewer system. Whether it would thrive is another question.

Personally, I love these stories. I love the "what ifs" and imagining all the possibilities. Whether these stories are concocted for fun, generated from practical jokes, or passed on as cultural oral histories, finding the origins of them can be fun and truly challenging.

Author and paranormal researcher Jeff Belanger has done extensive work in the area of legends. One in particular that he covered at a conference I attended was the Chupacabra. The translation from Spanish is "the goat-sucker." This name was first circulated in the mid-1990s; however, I would almost swear I heard about reported sightings of animals with similar descriptions of the Chupacabra in Central Texas in the late 1970s. I found this strange and researched it myself, because I was quite sure I knew about the Chupacabra my whole life. Oddly enough, I could not find any reference to the goat-sucker prior to the 1990s. Apparently, because I learned about the legend in the 1990s, and assumed it was an ancient Spanish legend, it had always been around. But I was wrong, and this legend proves that when dealing with the paranormal, fact checking is essential. But just because the name is different, does not mean the creature is fictional.

Official Records and Reports

Report details for paranormal events can be hard to come by and take some research. Other than governmental actions, tax, land records, and religious recordings of births or baptisms, day-to-day human events and interactions are not collectively stored anywhere. If it was significant, anything unusual was customarily passed on in the form of oral histories. Much of the mundane or unimportant activities people engaged in were simply not considered noteworthy and have disappeared and are lost forever. While the Industrial Revolution is said to begin around 1790 with the transition from handmade goods to machine-made goods, it wasn't until about 1900 that record keeping in the United States involved more than just names, dates, and actions. Because of advances in law, the sciences, anthropology, and history, record keeping became more and more detailed. Beginning around the 1920s, incidents reported to official government agencies or regulatory organizations included detailed accounts of the incident or issue in question. Usually, these accounts contained witnesses' names and sometimes more detailed information about their lives. Official reports recorded by city and county service departments, along with private organizations such as the Daughters of the American Revolution and Sons of Confederate Veterans, who operate genealogical research systems, are good places to search for historical information about people, places, and things. Many such organizations have access to death records that can support speculations about the cause of hauntings or paranormal experiences.

Governmental offices are great resources for specific kinds of records. Tax liens, land ownership deeds, marriages and divorces, births and deaths, military and civil service, all can be found by using the Freedom of Information Act. This process is relatively easy; each office will have their required procedures, and you need only ask. Unless you are searching for classified government information, just contact the government office that has authority over the records you seek and complete a written request for the documents you desire. Unfortunately, many records will be lost to time or poor records management, and there is nothing you can do about that. Also, if what you request is old, it will often be stored off site and there may be additional charges to retrieve it.

The Paper Trail

More often than not, local lore has no documentation foundation and cannot be verified. In Milam County, Texas, there is a community named Tanglewood. The name itself leads one to begin imagining some dreadful or mysterious story. In the early 1980s, the teenagers of Rockdale passed around a story about the Blackjack Monster. It was said that a carnival had traveled through Rockdale in the 1960s. It was one of those large carnivals with a midway of games, rides, caged wild animals, and oddities such as deformed persons and dead baby animals in formaldehyde-filled jars. The night before the carnival left, a black panther escaped from its cage and disappeared into the brambles of the Tanglewood forest. From then on, every scream in the night and every slain livestock carcass found was blamed on the Blackjack Monster.

The problem is, how do you investigate something a carnival might not report? If the carnival had reported it, the story would have been in all the papers or been filed in a police report. There was nothing. Once again, this is a no leads case. And the fact that the "monster" is still alive, stalking the cows and goats of Milam County, is a bit of a mystery in itself since the life expectancy of a panther is about 12 years.

However, like any good conspiracy theory, there is an explanation for that too; panthers and cougars can interbreed, thus creating a leap (group) of hybrid "couthers" running amok in the Tanglewood, screaming in the night and killing livestock. Could this have happened? My answer is—absolutely. Can we prove it by research? My answer is—doubtful. Does it matter enough to spend the time and money to try to capture one of the creatures? My answer is—no. So, we leave the Blackjack Monster to lore and allow the Tanglewood community to remain mysterious and move on to things we can prove—events that we can address and research and then make a determination.

Doing Your Homework

The following are productive avenues for conducting supportive research in your paranormal investigation:

Historical Society Research. Many communities, especially larger ones, have a historical society. These societies have a few people on payroll managing the records they keep and a volunteer force that helps run special events, searches for items and documents of historical value from the public record and may help run the society's day-to-day business.

Historical societies are valuable assets to the investigator or team. As an investigator, create a good working relationship with these folks; they will be invaluable to your research, potentially saving you scores of hours looking in the wrong place for information that may or may not exist.

When conducting research, you naturally make your way through the things that make sense to you, the things you believe to be related to the person, thing, or incident. That is where your searching will end and where the suggestions of the historical archivist or librarian will begin. They will have a different take on who and where you should search for information about your subject. Use their advice and see where it leads you. And, if they do come up with valuable information that is important to your discovery and goals, credit them for their help; they deserve it. If they think they are appreciated, they may look forward to working with you again, or may even send some more paranormal work your way.

Property Records Research. When a paranormal event is specifically found at a precise location, it is good practice to review the governmental records of that location. The local county appraisal district should have a complete history of who owned the property. This will be helpful for incidents supposedly originating within the last 200 years or so, some more, some less. In the Americas, obviously, you would usually not be able to discover who or what was on the property prior to European conquest unless ruins are present. In Texas, that could consist of middens (American Indian trash piles), Pueblo type construction in the southwest, and other types of structures throughout the United States. Once native occupation is confirmed, that influence has to remain a possibility of the origin of the paranormal occurrence.

Tax Roll Research. The county tax assessor collector's office will have similar information on file at the appraisal district office. This may show problems with the property such as liens, title clouds, foreclosures, etc. Such information indicates the possibility of intensified stress and may suggest the possibility of intense emotional events. This office will also have a running list of the owners of the property.

Family Records Research. As noted, letters, diaries, business receipts, recipes, family bibles, schoolwork, and other personal papers can be valuable evidentiary resources in your efforts to narrow down people, times, and places. A good working relationship with the family and the right kinds of questions may gain you access to grandma's stash of letters in the attic.

Business Records. Many businesses keep payroll records that will verify if a certain person worked at the business during a specified time. Supply records will validate equipment and particular structures or pieces of gear existing at the time of the "incident." You may discover service contracts that narrow down people, places, things, and services rendered to correlate with certain occurrences. However, because business records are private, the individuals who have control over those records must be cooperative.

Law Enforcement and Medical Examiner's Research. If you are investigating an event that would have been recorded by a law enforcement agency, go to that agency and file an open records request for the location or person. If the agency has records, they are compelled by federal law to provide them to you, unless the case is still open or unsolved. Obviously, the age of the investigation will determine the availability and the detail of these records.

Court Research. The county and district clerk's offices serve as clerks of the court for all criminal and civil courts, including commissioners' court and probate court. They maintain the official records of the courts they serve. Many records in these offices are kept on microfiche. Research can be tedious; however, these records, including probate, can be very useful for filling in gaps and developing chronological timelines.

Hospital Records Research. Due to recently passed medical privacy laws, hospital records are extremely difficult to obtain. Even records of deceased patients from state hospitals, for example, are subject to censure. In most cases, hospital records would need to come from family sources.

Cemetery Research. In many cases, older cemeteries may no longer keep records or even have records. There are many private and family cemeteries that are considered abandoned. In those cases, your only real choice is to seek out any cemetery historical societies in the area or revert to the county clerk's office for probate rulings and official death records.

Census Research. It has been my experience that using a company like Ancestry.com or MyHeritage.com pays for itself in gas and time alone. Census data is extremely complex to research and companies like these have already done the work for you and may be able to take you right to the person you are searching for. After all, the latest census counted 300-plus million in the United States alone, and that's not counting all the deceased's records back to the time of the person you are searching for. Unless you have unlimited time, I suggest you go to an online source, pay for the information and be done with it.

Genealogy Research. In the past four months, I have learned more about my own family than I have known in my entire life. I encourage you to go through online resources such as (1) Ancestry.com, (2) MyHeritage.com, and (3) 23andMe.com (DNA testing). I have tracked my family's records, both maternally and paternally, almost to the 1500s. My DNA strains track me to Ireland on my mother's side and Sardinia on my father's side and even further to almost 35,000 years ago where the line began. And, yes, as you may have guessed, I am 3% Neanderthal, my greatest accomplishment!

When researching family matters, yours or your clients, I encourage you to seek out such sources and capitalize on the research already done. Why reinvent the wheel?

Internet Research. When using the Internet, there are many verified sources with accurate information. However, there are a lot of sites that your standard search engine will direct you to where you may find the information questionable. Be careful what you take as fact off the Internet, unless it comes from scrutinized or peer reviewed sources.

Unofficial Citizen Records

One of the most overlooked resources are family records. Determine if there are family members, possibly older, who can corroborate the story. Then ask if these older family members have any records or personal letters to support the information. These writings can be a treasure trove of information.

My grandmother, Sarah Adams Lawson, had two sons, Bruce Adams Lawson and William Clayton Lawson. They were born over a decade apart and were raised separately, never really getting to know one another. Both served in the US Army during World War II, Clayton in the US Army Signal Corps and Bruce in the US Army Air Corps. Sarah saved all the letters her sons sent to her in two large fabric swatch books from which she had removed the cloth samples. While military intelligence screeners cut out much of the details from their letters, they were a superior source of information to what, when, and where these two men were engaged. Letters, diaries, business receipts, recipes, family bibles, schoolwork, and other personal papers can be valuable evidentiary resources in your efforts to narrow down people, times, and places.

Unproductive Information and False Leads

In just about every investigation, there will be unproductive intelligence. The information can originate from a well-intentioned citizen, an intentionally misleading sociopath, or something in between. The question is, what motivates the person to provide you with clues to your mystery? Everyone has an incentive. Either they truly want to help, they want recognition, they want profit, or they want to influence the process. If you can determine their motivation, you will be able to better understand them and identify good information.

EXAMPLE: The Telephone Clairvoyant—Austin, Texas

In 2007 through 2010, I assisted in several murder investigations. For one of the investigations, I had provided information to Crime Stoppers and was the person to contact after the TV show aired the information. At this point, we were looking only for information from anyone who happened to be in the area of the murder and may have seen something not immediately recognized as criminal in nature. The first day I received about 40 calls. The second day, maybe 30. The third day less than 10. Out of all of them, most were people who drove by the murder location and just wanted to help. However, three were obviously conspiracy theorists and possibly psychotic. They had called multiple times, leaving lengthy, run-on messages about religious and ceremonial death rites, long haul truck driver serial killers, and a cartel murder hit. One of these people called repeatedly because she felt we had not done enough, and I was not doing what she told me. During an active investigation, you never want to reveal your core facts. In this case, I ultimately had to tell her she was completely wrong and delusional. I advised her to seek treatment and ended our conversation. I was lucky to know certain things about the case; had I been aware of no additional information about the investigation, I would have been forced to follow up on her religious sacrifice leads. We would have wasted hours.

Unfortunately, circumstances dictate you may have nothing better to go on than the limited information you initially receive. In those situations, you have to work with what you have. Many paranormal incidents are like that; exaggerations, embellishments, and assumptions have been passed from person to person and story to story. Separating the significant from the insignificant is sometimes impossible. If something is possible and you have nothing to disprove it, you have to follow it up. Time is your enemy. You need to become adept at recognizing and eliminating unproductive information so you can move on to the truth.

CHAPTER 14

Beyond the TV Paradigm

What most people know about law is based on TV crime scene and detective shows. Even well-trained police officers fall into the primetime trap. With strong education and years of experience, officers know better than to have a suspect put their hands on a vehicle or other fixed object during a pat down search; the suspect can use the object as leverage to push off and try to assault or escape from the officer. I have personally experienced this. But time and time again, they will do it. When you ask why, they will say they don't know why they instructed the suspect to do so. But I know why. It is because they have much more visual training through watching TV than the five pat-down scenarios they participated in while in police training. It is estimated that upon graduation from high school, a person has received thousands more hours of social and behavioral instruction from TV than from their formal high school classroom instruction.

Reality vs. Television

If you have not watched the movie *Galaxy Quest*, you need to. It is the finest spoof on the *Star Trek*© series ever attempted. In a nutshell, an alien race has been receiving the television broadcasts from Earth to include *Gilligan's Island*, *Star Trek*©, and many others. They believe these "documentaries" to be true and recreate their entire society after the *Galaxy Quest/Star Trek*© example. While it is a great premise to model yourself or your organization after a successful mentor, you should first establish a goal for that model. Don't get me wrong, I have had the pleasure of interviewing, interacting with, or working alongside investigators on very successful TV shows. I am merely asking the question: Are you making a TV ghost hunting show or conducting a paranormal investigation? From my perspective, they are two different things.

CASE STUDY: Four Nights at the Vinoy Hotel—St. Petersburg, Florida

So there I was, at a Department of Justice Homicide Investigators' Conference in St. Petersburg, Florida. I was walking into the lobby of the Vinoy Hotel with my wife Lynn, also known as my Behavior Modification Unit (BMU). I had geared up for a weeklong conference and was looking forward to learning more about major crimes investigations. I wasn't paying attention to the check-in process, just kind of scanning the lobby and taking it all in.

Lynn asked the clerk, "Is room 521 available?"

I thought this was odd and stopped my wandering to listen to their conversation.

The clerk stared at her, puzzled. "It is always available," she said.

"We would like that one."

The clerk entered our information into the computer. "I have to tell you that if you want to move out of the room later, we cannot give you a credit, and we will have to charge you for an additional room."

"That's okay," Lynn said.

"What are we talking about?" I asked.

Lynn said, "It was featured on *Ghost Hunters;* it's haunted."

The clerk made an apologetic face and shrugged. "If there are problems, and you want to change rooms, there will be a fee."

In unison we said, "Okay."

We grabbed our suitcases and headed to the room.

Once there, we unpacked and then set up the computer to watch the *Ghost Hunters'* investigation of the Vinoy. In a nutshell, two of the *Ghost Hunters* team spent the night in room 521 and the core facts they came away with were these: (1) a light flickering, (2) closet doors opening, (3) ironing board falling off the wall, and (4) moaning. Luckily, each of these occurrences could easily be isolated and observed.

Since I had not brought any of my equipment, I chose to employ about 100 movement detectors in the room. These comprised of yellow, green, red, orange, and clear original Gummy Bears. I placed them strategically throughout the room to indicate if anything moved without our assistance. (Hey, don't judge, make do with what you have.) Oddly, four days later, none of the Gummies had moved; however, most of the green ones had disappeared—oddly they are Lynn's favorite flavor... I took a good look at the Mechanisms of Paranormal Indicators (MPI). These are physical objects purported to be "affected" by paranormal influences. In this case, the MPIs would be the doors, the ironing board hanger and ironing board, the table lamp, and noises. Here is how I addressed each issue:

The doors. The closet opening closures are constructed of two outward swinging doors, one to the right and one to the left. They are on standard hinges and when closed are secured with a single, metal, spring-loaded ball-catch. When used, both doors swing freely without a sound. Each ball-catch operated very smoothly to provide easy access when opening. The hinges and ball-catches were fairly new or at least well maintained to minimize noise when opening and closing. A forceful bump along the center frame of the door would cause the doors to open.

The ironing board and mount. The ironing board was a standard collapsible style constructed of lightweight metal with a cloth covering. It was intended to be mounted with a standard ironing board metal wall bracket, inside the center of the left wall of the closet. This wall is an exterior wall and the interior corner of the wall is connected to the exterior corner of the outside hallway, where the fireproof door is mounted, providing access to the fire escape. The wall-mounting bracket had two metal rods shaped like half hooks designed to hold the ironing board footings. One of the hooks was slightly bent, though I do not believe it was bent enough to have caused the ironing board to fall. However, if someone was not particularly careful, and quickly hung the board without taking care that both footings were properly placed into the holders, it could be knocked loose from a slight impact on the wall.

The table lamp. The table lamp was of metal and ceramic construction. Assuming it was the same one as in the episode, I checked the cord, the light socket, the inside cord connections, and the housing switch. I noticed nothing unusual about the lamp to indicate that it would be prone to malfunctions. While it was on, I wiggled the cord, light bulb and socket, turned it upside down, and shook it. None of this made the light flicker.

Other mechanical things. I checked the sink faucets, and tub and shower controls; all appeared to be in good working order. I checked the firmness of the electrical socket connections using my laptop cord plug; all were secure. I checked the cords on the TV and other lamps. And I checked the ventilation, which appeared to function properly.

To specifically address these mechanisms, I (1) left the closet doors open, (2) took the ironing board off the holder, and (3) ensured the lamp was properly connected, then went about normally.

Hotel Background

Built in 1925 as a luxury seasonal hotel, the Vinoy has an impressive history of tenants, to include Calvin Coolidge, Babe Ruth, and Marilyn Monroe. Its colorful past, involving the initial construction, existence through the WWII years, and its premature closing and abandonment in 1974, has given rise to several legends. The most famous one is the "Woman in White." She is said to roam the halls and has been seen by more than one professional baseball player and other guests staying at the venue. She is believed to be the restless spirit of Elsie Elliott, a worldly socialite. It is said that her well-to-do land baron husband, Eugene Elliott, shoved her down a flight of stairs. However, some believe the Woman in White is actually the ghost of Elsie's personal servant who had previously witnessed Elsie's murder and was scheduled to provide testimony to the facts she had witnessed. But, before she was able to testify in court, she mysteriously disappeared. Guests have reported water faucets turning on, toilets flushing, and electrical disturbances.

Our Experiences

During our stay at the Vinoy, we experienced only one of the four indicators identified in the *Ghost Hunters* episode: voices. I should actually say, moaning.

The second night there, as we were about to retire for the evening, both Lynn and I felt a certain energy about the room. A liveliness that was not there before. There seemed to be a vibration in the structure that was unusual. We talked about it and it intensified for a moment, and then went silent. After several minutes, the vibration was back. After about another 20 minutes it suddenly intensified again, then went silent. This was creepy. I turned on the light, put on my khaki shorts and began checking the room. The wall at the head of the bed was definitely vibrating, very quietly, but it was there. If you closed your eyes and listened, you could hear moaning, just like Charles Dickens' Ghost of Christmas Past, low and breathy. I checked the closet doors; they too were vibrating. The ironing board sat motionless and silent on the floor. I checked the inside of the closet; the vibration intensified to a loud thump, the closet walls vibrated and intensely shook for just a moment, and then went silent. After several seconds, the moaning started again. I put my ear against the closet wall and could hear it better. Definite vibration and definite moaning.

At this point, I really thought the Vinoy staff was playing a trick on us. I whispered Lynn I was going to check the hall. I slipped out into the hallway by myself. I walked to the left, to the end of the hall, which would be the closet corner of our room, next to what was a fire-safe door. This door led to the fire escape, and judging by its construction design and material, was added after the main building was constructed. I opened the fire-safe door and there was a gust of wind that escaped, and a strong breeze could be felt from outside. I walked onto the fire escape landing and stood for a moment. The fire escape is made out of both solid and hollow concrete masonry brick units held together with cement. The construction appeared to be separate from the original building and the masonry wall joints are sealed with some form of flexible latex and tar-like material. The fire escape has two landings for each floor and the opposite, exterior walls have a hollow brick design that allows outside air into the escape. I let go of the fire-safe door to allow it to close. Powered by its hydraulic closing mechanism, it began its slow closing movement. Approximately three to five inches away from being totally closed, the door slammed shut, vibrating the exterior wall and ensuring the door was secured and locked within its metal doorframe.

I stood on the landing and listened. Slowly the air pressure in the fire escape began to lessen due to the strong winds coming off the beach, and the moaning returned. I walked down to the second landing, between the fifth and fourth floors, and could feel the suction through the hollow brick design, caused by the exterior winds from the beach. The entire fire escape's construction is akin to a giant vertical flute with open holes along its body. When all of the fire-safe doors are closed, if the wind comes from the proper direction it passes over the holes just like someone blowing on the opening of a bottle, producing a low-toned moan. As I stood on the second landing, the fire-safe door from the fifth floor opened and two couples entered. Immediately, they paused at seeing a very white, barefoot guy wearing nothing more than a pair of khaki shorts, standing silent and motionless in the shadows between floors. Without a word, wide-eyed they stopped, bumped into each other, turned around, exited the fire escape and went for the elevator down the hall. The door closed slowly as the pressure equalized, then shut with a thump.

I often wonder if those two couples have their own Vinoy ghost tale about the "The Shadow Man in Khaki."

Competency vs. Ratings: Is There a Balance?

It is a simple fact; attractiveness helps ratings. Would you rather have Kris Williams from *Ghost Hunters* explaining the paranormal investigation or crazy Uncle Jesse from the *Dukes of Hazzard*? Okay, your crazy uncle might be a bit more entertaining around the campfire, but as far as credibility and the ability to tell a chronological and concise account of the investigative events, Kris would win that contest. However, is that why she was initially employed for TV? Was it because of her expertise in professional investigations, parapsychology, or for her experience with the paranormal? I have spoken with her about these things and the answer is, no. She got the job because of her talent and ability to professionally explain ideas and actions in front of a camera and based on what TV producers would unknowingly use: The Conscious Patzer Effect. I will explain. The Conscious Patzer Effect is the automatic tendency to attribute expertise and trustworthiness to physically attractive people. Like it or not, it is true. It is the same when we hear the guy from *Dirty Jobs* explain how the universe works. I am pretty sure he didn't do all the physics calculations to determine the output of the flux capacitor, yet we trust what he is telling us because we have the preconceived idea to do so, because we like his voice. In Kris' case, she gained most of her expertise in the field after joining *Ghost Hunters*, not before. Now considered a true professional in the realm of paranormal research, she has become the total package, attractive with truly established credibility.

And that is the trick, to be able to determine the credibility of someone whose appearance makes them look non-credible. This happens every day in law enforcement investigations. Just because someone appears to lack credibility does not mean the evidence and testimony they put forth are not credible. The evidence and testimony should be scrutinized, not the person's history or lack of expertise or experience. However, in order to interpret an investigative outcome and render an opinion, a person must have certifiable expert training and experience. That is what TV has as a real challenge, along with creating an exciting show. The problem is, proper research, as Kris will tell you, does not make for action-packed TV.

The Real Question is: Are the facts being presented, or are the interesting parts being blown out of proportion and then becoming the facts?

The Effects of Time on TV Programing

If there is anything I understand, it is time pressure. It affects all people differently; some people thrive in it, others crumble. After military parachuting and civilian skydiving for over 20 years, I understand there is a limited amount of time to get things done or catastrophic consequences can occur. In the realm of compressed time, "smooth is fast." In law enforcement, probably nothing is more time sensitive than conducting a vehicle assault. A suspect is in a vehicle that has the capability of driving, and due to whatever circumstances, an impending threat of suicide, taking of a hostage, threat of continued aggression, or any number of other things, the burden of deciding on securing the driver is imminent. To take action or to not take action, that is the question. Either decision could result in disastrous consequences.

Demanding filming schedules for TV shows may not be as physically perilous, but they are certainly dangerous when it comes to the ending of TV careers. As most paranormal investigators know, real research and investigation is about as boring for TV viewers as watching paint dry. Seriously. At least when you are waiting for water to boil, something is for sure going to happen. The stress put on the creators of shows like *Ghost Hunters* and others is incredible. Finding locations, getting the background, going to the site, setting up for filming, conducting the investigation, pulling out, and then editing the recordings to fit the TV timeline in order to gain or maintain ratings is an ulcer-producing process. These demands are not conducive to conducting a proper and thorough investigation. Therefore, it is so important for paranormal investigative groups to have at least three sections within their organization. And remember, one person can be assigned multiple positions.

1. Management Section
2. Research Section
3. Investigation Section

The ideal setup for a paranormal group manages these requirements and delegates them to other individuals in the group. The Central Texas Paranormal Detectives have a structure in which the historian, researcher, and scribe rarely go to the investigative scene. They maintain a pristine relationship to the investigation based solely on documentation research and recording. This method helps to eliminate any external influences among the members. It also elevates members who would rather be ghost hunting from the mundane and tedious work of sorting through old jail logs, death records, and newspaper articles.

A paranormal investigation should strive to be more of an extended case study than a one or two night tromp through a condemned mental hospital. Although, that would be fun and can result in recording experiences.

Budget Constraints

TV is not just about entertainment, and it is not just about the research. Ultimately, it is about the money. How much will it cost to produce a show and how much will the show make in profits? The *Blair Witch Project* is a great example of what can be done with very little. Many TV shows have modeled their productions from this, hence the popularity of reality TV programs. I have a friend who works in a nature-based reality show. The interesting aspect of the progression of many of the reality-based shows is that the more popular the show, the more money the participants (actors) require. Thus, the more the participants are dropped from the show and replaced with less expensive participants. It seems the nature of things. So, bottom line, following the money seems to dictate who and what happens.

TV producers are not the only ones who have budget constraints; even Michael Dell, the founder of Dell Computer, has a budget. I know paranormal groups have theirs. The travel, lodging, research, and equipment all have their costs. In order for a group to lessen the stress of raising and managing funds, several considerations must be addressed. Some questions are: should you have a treasurer? Should you register as a non-profit? Or should everyone be responsible for their own stuff? Whatever the group decides, it will still be useful to develop a set of operational guidelines in order to address these issues and suppress potential bickering.

Ghost Hunting vs. Ghost Investigating

It is all in the perspective. The mind-set. Once again, are you *Scooby Doo* or *Ghostbusters*? The TV show *Ghost Hunters* is very correctly named; they are ghost hunters. They conduct brief research endeavors, determine if there is anomalous activity, insert themselves, record what they find, and move on. Others would also define "ghost hunting" as simply going to a location without any record of previous paranormal activity to identify a haunting or other phenomena that no one before has discovered. This is the actual hunting. We do this in cemeteries and around old abandoned buildings every day.

A true paranormal investigation is something more in depth. It is the whole package. The identification and recording of a real history, of the legend, of capturing the paranormal experience, and of presenting credible evidence of the experience interpreted by reasonable people. This is a different level of investigation. This is being a paranormal detective.

Formula to Creating Drama

It certainly helps to have predictable and imaginative people to guide a ghost story. Many of these folks say the reason most people never see ghosts or phenomena is because they do not open their minds to it. This may very well be true; I do not doubt that there is more to the paranormal than taking a digital recording of it. However, being open to phenomena and misinterpreting a natural event are two different things. Furthermore, actually creating phenomena is simply irresponsible. Like any other formula to drama, paranormal drama consists of the setup, the buildup, and the payoff. For some ghost program TV watchers, the payoff is the discovery of phenomena. For some it is the adventure. And for some it is the spoof of having a completely awkward believer get the pants scared off of him.

CASE EXAMPLE: The Organizer, Name and Location Withheld

I was asked by a friend to participate in an event in Austin. I responded to the location and met with them. There were network TV people on site along with several other paranormal investigators, one of whom had been instrumental in organizing the documentation of this event. We will call this person The Organizer. While introductions were made, The Organizer felt the need to speak with me at length. I knew much of the background about the location and was entertained with the explanation of the events as he told it. Their details were right on, and I was interested as they moved forward with the taping of the event. The Organizer seemed to decide that he had not sufficiently convinced me of the legitimacy of this paranormal event, so they brought out a dowsing instrument. They asked that I sit down at the table and witness their communication with the dead. They dangled a crystal pendulum on a metal chain and allowed it to settle straight down.

"Is anyone in the spirit world present?" they asked, or something like that. I witnessed them slightly roll the chain between their index finger and thumb and the instrument began to swing to and fro in the direction they wanted. Then they said, "Stop," and the swinging immediately stopped, as they very slightly lowered the chain and brought it back to its original level. They asked, "Are you a man or a woman?" The crystal began a side-to-side motion as they used their middle finger to bring the chain back to life again. "A woman," they said.

I leaned forward and very quietly said, "You understand I am a cop, right?" Hoping he would understand that I was adept at spotting fraud and that I could clearly see he was controlling how the crystal would swing. I was hoping he would cease the theatrics, but he simply continued. I have witnessed mediums and spiritualist use all manners of dowsing instruments to help people in search of answers, the locations for paranormal hotspots, and to talk with the dead. This was not one of those times.

The evening proceeded and I merely observed. The Organizer was busy taking pictures with a digital camera and, out of every four or five shots, they would point out faces and body shapes in the digital viewer. I could not make out a single definable shape they described the whole night. And there were orbs everywhere. The Organizer was completely delighted with them; this is a 100 plus year-old structure with open ventilation and open, truss-type overhead rafters. Tendrils of cobwebs drifted like ocean seaweed from the beams.

I escaped and went into an adjacent room and took a series of five pictures of the room on my iPhone. Then I walked to the light fixture hanging above a table and thumped it with my middle finger. I waited several minutes and took five more pictures from the same vantage point. And yes, you guessed correctly, I got orbs. And I got a couple of skyfish and flying rods as well; apparently there were some gnats nestled up in the light fixture too.

Let me say this, once and for all, I am not a debunker. I am a detective, an inter-disciplinarian, an instructional technologist, a specialist in complex-adaptive-systems, and an observer of human behavior and performance. I want more than anything for paranormal investigators to be correct about their findings. But it is my job to determine whether or not the reportee believes what they have experienced is real and whether the phenomena can be explained conventionally. Once those two questions have been addressed, you will have your answer.

CHAPTER 15

Historical vs. Contemporary Reporting

For events reported before the 1900s, newspapers are the go-to for information possibly related to your paranormal investigation. In Austin, Texas, we are fortunate to have a very well-organized and eager historical society to help unravel those local urban legends and reported hauntings. Most of the historical reporting data will have to stand on its own and cannot be independently corroborated. Such records often lead investigators into the realm of wild speculation and can influence you to veer off the path of facts and onto the rough and rocky road of imagination. Granted, having a good imagination is needed to be a good investigator. When in check, that imagination helps to clearly see things that are related and identify unknown relationships.

Understanding Historical Context

When I was a mental health officer in the late 1980s, I was assigned to investigate persons suspected of having a mental illness, psychotic episodes, or manifesting abnormal behavior attributed to critical stress or ideas of suicide. Mental health officers are trained to recognize the signs and symptoms of mental illness, what it is and what it isn't. Delusions of grandeur to indicate manic behavior, auditory and visual hallucinations indicate someone may be schizophrenic, or odd or defiant behavior indicate someone is simply a jerk.

In some cases, the abnormal behavior is attributed to drugs. The mental health officer must determine whether or not the behavior was due to current drug intoxication or to a physical condition known as drug-induced psychosis. If the subject is actually under the influence, no matter how disturbed, it becomes a law enforcement matter. If they are not intoxicated, it's classified as a mental health matter. The exception lies in their cognitive state, and whether it is deemed a mental condition rather than an illness, such as having a head injury, brain lesions, brain tumor, dementia, Alzheimer's, epilepsy, or other physical causes. In addition, mental health officers are trained in mental health law, suicide mediation, and sometimes hostage negotiation.

At the time I was in mental health, we answered all mental health calls in the county and cities. On midnight shifts, when it was slow, I would go to the admissions office at the Austin State Hospital and hang out with the admissions staff and on-call psychiatrist. If it were really slow, I would get the keys to the main building, which was condemned for renovation at the time, and walk around in the basement—at night—by myself—with a flashlight. This is the same basement that a century ago housed the sickest of the sick, who were committed to what was then known as the State Lunatic Asylum. Built in 1857, this building was the warehouse for the truly disturbed. Thousands of people were committed behind those walls and suffered all manner of barbarism and torture. When I strolled the corridors, all the doors had been removed from the patient cells and were propped up next to the door openings. Inside these small rooms were stacks and stacks of record boxes, to which I had free access. Of the records I read from the 1880s, most patients admitted into the State Lunatic Asylum were referred for religious concerns, chronic masturbation, or consumption (tuberculosis). Most of the records I scanned did not indicate a treatment, just the physical condition and mental behavior. However, we can only assume that the treatment was much like every other lunatic asylum where the incarcerated were chained to walls, cribbed, bled, spun, electrocuted, submerged in ice and freezing water, put in restraint and tranquilizer chairs, and displayed to the public for entertainment.

Such treatments for handling the insane were common in the United States. One of the best accounts of this type of "care" was recorded by journalist Nellie Bly in her 1887 book, *10 Days in a Madhouse*. Nellie posed as a mental patient to get committed and recorded her and others' treatment while she posed as a patient at Blackwell's Island Insane Asylum in New York.

If there are any places on Earth that would meet all the criteria necessary to make a reasonable person believe they could be haunted, insane asylums would be at the top of the list. The main building at the Austin State Hospital is certainly one of these.

Since then, the main building has been renovated and serves as administrative offices for the hospital. In past years, it was a featured stop on Austin's Haunted ATX Hearse Tours. However, policies at the state hospital have changed, and now no one is allowed on the grounds for anything but hospital-related business.

I know, you're still thinking about the chronic "masturbation" thing... Me too. But, of the records I reviewed, many of them assigned more modern diagnosis and treatments, but still remained barbaric by today's standards. Nearing the year 1900, many of the diagnoses morphed into subsections of either moral or physical maladies Moral maladies being those behaviors due to social dysfunction, such as domestic abuse, worry, and overwork. The physical pertained to diseases of the brain, psychological mental illnesses, injuries to the head, and yes, masturbation, again...The interesting thing is that while I was a mental health officer for two years, I only had one person who I could say would have fit the criteria for hospitalization for masturbation. No, not me... He was a drifter I did an emergency commitment on who apparently could not stop himself. I had wondered why, 100 years ago, so many were put into mental hospitals for this behavior, and so few today. I researched further and realized that many of the behaviors and experiences that mental patients exhibit are contemporary, meaning they directly relate to their own times, current events, and technology. Prior to photography being common, the only way a depraved man could see a woman would be window peeping or being in the proximity of a woman, to become aroused.

I have been in law enforcement since 1986 and have never taken a window peeping call; that's not to say it doesn't happen. This type of behavior has evolved into internet pornographic addictions that are seldom public in nature. The same goes for much of religion. The reports of Jesus complexes have declined dramatically in lieu of delusions of grandeur of corporate CEOs, powerful politicians and people that report extraterrestrial experiences. According to articles in *The Guardian, The Catholic News Agency,* and *The Catholic Herald,* demonic possession is on the increase for religious believers. Both the Catholic Church and The Church of England have increased their exorcism training and assignments of priests to investigate demonic possession. However, since the 1960s there has been an increase of reported CIA mind control and NSA surveillance bugging and spying accusations from those that do not have strong religious beliefs.

An individual's consciousness is affected by the information that is taken into the brain and encoded into memory. Most of this information being from present-day happenings and experiences. Therefore, mental illness is more likely to manifest itself in a modern way and according to the beliefs of the experiencer. The odd thing, according to an article written by Fr. Alexander Lucie-Smith in the April 2018 issue of *The Catholic Herald,* titled "Belief in God is declining, but belief in the devil remains strong" he asserts believing in God or the devil is not mutually exclusive. The concept is more along the lines of the struggle between good and evil and society's belief that evil-doers will be brought to justice. But, whatever the cause, the paranormal investigator should be as well informed about mental illness and cultural beliefs as about the supernatural.

Records in Perspective

It is important to be aware of correlating information when conducting research. Investigators should strive to understand the perspective of the person who wrote the account so many years ago. Their interpretation of the event will be explained through their limited experience. Without knowledge of correlations, you can be sidetracked. While Bible quotes are highly arguable, I will briefly discuss one example: Lot's wife turning into a pillar of salt. If one were not familiar with the saying "he was so scared, he turned into a pillar of salt," one would think Lot's wife did in fact become salt. On the contrary, it can be like a northerner saying, "It scared me so much, I froze." Or it could be what the ancient astronaut theorist Zecharia

Sitchin postulates, that the salt reference was simply a mistranslation from Hebrew and merely meant she disappeared like salt dissolved in water. At this point, which theorist can prove they are correct?

Experience is Individualistic

Each person's understanding is based on personal experiences with the world. Dealing with history, hundreds of other people's accounts, requires extensive knowledge to understand a single written account of an incident. Metaphor and exaggeration must be identified and placed into the context for the time. Could you imagine living in a time where the only things you know are what you personally experience? Today, we are exposed to hundreds of times more information than our forbearers, stories in books, TV, magazines, music, and the Internet. When reading historical accounts that predate modern information technology, take into consideration the witness's or writer's limited world. While their perspective may lean toward a bias, the location typically will not. You as the investigator should be able to separate the person's views from the location, and vet the location's credibility on its own.

Remember, facts written by historical writers will differ from those written by current writers.

CHAPTER 16

Vetting the Location

Haunted lore is usually passed down through a mixture of factual history and exaggeration. In many cases, as with the Ghost Wagon of Westlake Hills, several stories are merged into one. Travelers will take these stories and transplant them along their way or at their destination.

Story Morph and Migration

People hearing tales for the first time usually get the main characters and idea of the story but will later fill in the portions they did not remember. Determining the origin of lore is of paramount significance in order to confirm the validity of the event to be investigated.

EXAMPLE: Crybaby Bridge—Apache Pass, Texas

This took place one night in 1980, when I was 16 years old, and my dear friend Ricky Williams was 18. We were driving in his cherry-red 1968 Camaro. There were a couple of full bottles of Mickey's malt liquor still left in the cooler and we were hauling ass (driving fast) down County Road 908 near what is now known as Apache Pass. He hung a right onto County Road 428, a red-clay-and-gravel road covered with the outstretched limbs of blackjack and pecan trees; it was like racing through a tunnel. The road abruptly curved to the right and headed toward the San Gabriel River.

Ricky slammed on his brakes, and we slid sideways, stopping right at the edge of the bridge that spanned the river. A cloud of dirt and rocks flew past us in the car's headlights, and then slowly the structure came into view. In front, but slightly off to the side, was a rusted iron and rotted wood, trestle-style bridge. It extended over the sandy-loam banks of the San Gabriel. Live oaks and pecan trees fingered through the top openings of the trestles in nature's attempt to reclaim what was once hers. Ricky shut off the car and got out. I followed as the car's lights still illuminated the banks.

"Have you ever been here?" he asked.

"Nope." I took a swig of my Mickey's.

He walked out onto the weathered oaken boards that made up the actual bridge. The rest of what would be the road was intentionally missing, exposing the support structures underneath. "This is Crybaby Bridge," he said.

Carefully, I stepped out onto the wooden walkway near the side of the railing. The railing was made of nothing more than round runs of iron and old rivets, most of which were missing. "I've heard of it. Why do they call it Crybaby Bridge?"

As he walked out, he explained, "A long time ago, there was some guy, his wife and their kid driving along out here. I think he was taking the kid to the doctor or something. He was driving too fast, and when they came across the bridge, one of his wheels ran off the wood runner and it flipped the car and they ended up down there." He threw his Mickey's bottle down and it hit the roof of an old 1930s-style car that lay smashed in the water. The green glass shattered everywhere and flickered in the headlights of Ricky's car.

I looked down at the car. "Who were they?"

"I don't know!" he said, irritated. "Who cares? The point is the father and mother lived. They climbed out of the car and tried to find the baby. The water was higher then, not like now, and they say they could hear the baby crying, but could never find it. And if you come out here, and are very quiet, you can still hear the baby."

"Were they—"

"Shut up and listen," Ricky said.

And I did.

We stood for a long time. Then there was a slight breeze that flexed the tree limbs a bit, just enough to move the edges of the leaves on the trestle iron beams. A breeze strong enough to make the old skeleton of the bridge shift slightly but enough to carry the sound of a baby crying to my ears, ever so soft, for a moment.

Ricky reached over, grabbed my Mickey's bottle from me, chugged it down, and threw it onto the hood of the car below. "Let's get out of here."

And we did.

I loved Crybaby Bridge. From that point on I went out there practically every weekend. Bored driving back and forth between the Wal-Mart, Sonic, Pizza Hut, and Brookshire Brothers grocery, I, or we, would head out to the bridge and sit, drink, swim and whatever. I heard the baby cry a hundred times, but I never looked for him.

What we didn't know is that Crybaby Bridge spanned the San Gabriel River near Apache Pass, a gravel bar that made it easy to ford the water, even when it was high. It was a place where, 230 years prior in the 1750s, long before Texas revolted against Mexico, Spanish soldiers and priests crossed the water to get to their missions and presidio on the then-named San Xavier River and a smaller tributary known only as The Brook of the Souls. Here the Spanish ministered to and abused the native Indian tribes of the Caddo, Lipan, Tonkawa and others. And it was here that in reprisal, a Catholic priest and another missionary were murdered inside the mission itself. These are the kinds of historical facts that a good researcher can gather out of mysterious lore. While we were focusing on Crybaby Bridge, other things were truly there. Things we missed.

Several years later, when I was in the Army stationed at Fort Bragg, I found out that there was a Crybaby Bridge in Raeford, North Carolina, also. And one in Milford, Virginia; Eagle River, Alaska; and Shelton, Washington. Apparently, anywhere an old trestle bridge tends to get blown by the wind, there is a Crybaby Bridge.

Knowing the Lore

Vetting your location is especially important when you are trying to conduct a professional paranormal investigation. Most paranormal activity is incredibly hard to track down and even harder to prove. Once you get the story, hit the internet and find out if your tale has a twin. When you get a story of a location and head out to find the ghost, it might be fun, but do you really know what you are looking for? In Crybaby-Bridge-like cases, one of the first things a paranormal investigator should do is obtain the address of the incident, work out an approximate year of the incident, and then search death records to see if anything will match up with the story. This is easily done with surviving records after the 1890s.

Blind Testing

Several years ago, I watched a TV show where the producers checked a location to ensure it was devoid of any event possibly considered paranormal in nature. A wood frame house was built, made to look old, and the show sent unsuspecting people in to test their psychic ability. All participants but one claimed feeling some strange force inside the house. A couple of the participants identified the spirit of a dead person there, and one even formulated a story about the deceased person they thought occupied the house. Afterward, the producers informed everyone of the ruse. None could explain the forces they felt or the imagery they conjured in this brand new, never-occupied stage prop. And no, they did not use wood from an old home, this was all newly milled wood from the lumberyard. But we can still take into consideration those unknowns of the land where the house was built or that an item or person was there with an attached spirit. That is the tricky thing about trying to make sense of paranormal events, especially when the evidence you are relying on comes from the brain and emotions of a human. With that said, never discount the experience. There could be something to why they had the experiences they did.

A good experiment within a team would be to have several people research a site and not allow the investigators to know what they are looking for. The result becomes unmolested evidence of the experience. There would be no way for the investigator to talk themselves into the event, because they know nothing about it.

Putting the Dots Together

I once consulted with a paranormal group on a vetting issue. The team leader had spoken with a homeowner who reported several instances of phenomena in her residence. She had lived in the house for over 10 years with no complaint. In the spring of 2012, she began to notice small gray areas out of the corners of her eyes. When she would turn to look, they would be gone. There were light and electrical disturbances throughout the house and standard TV distortions that I recognized as magnetic interference but from an unknown source. I knew I would have to address degaussing the TV (removing the interfering magnetic field) and identify the magnetism or electromagnetic fluctuations in the residence.

The team had already researched the property, house, and builder, and there was no history to indicate a cause for paranormal activity. At this point, following my general advice, they decided to forgo the investigation. The team leader told me he was going to suggest the homeowner see an optometrist for her eyes, an electrician for her home's wiring, and get a new TV. At that point, if the problems persisted, he would come in and do an investigation.

I applauded the team leader for his critical thinking but told him he took my advice of intense research prior to the investigation too far. Eliminating the known causes of anomalies does not mean the anomalies are not paranormal in nature. While he had checked to see if any deaths had occurred on the property, he had not checked the deaths of all persons who ever occupied the property and had not acquired personal information about the homeowner, such as a recent spiritual involvement, the purchase of new home furnishings, or external personal changes in relationships, career, or recreation. He was puzzled, and I expanded. I asked if it was possible that the homeowner purchased used furniture with a spirit imprint on the item. I asked if she had recently engaged in any kind of spirit activity that could have opened her to a dangerous entity, or if she had had recent employment stressors in her life that could lead to paranormal interpretation. Several weeks went by before I heard back from the team leader. He had researched further and connected two pieces of this puzzle: (1) In 2012, the homeowner had picked up a part-time job as a kids' party clown, and (2) a child who had resided at the residence in the 1970s died after the family moved to another city. These two facts could lead one to inquire whether the presence of a clown in a home could somehow trigger a reaction for a child ghost who had returned to the home where she had an emotional attachment. While this may be a loose association, it would nonetheless provide some form of foundation in which to begin a real paranormal investigation. Otherwise, the phenomena might be viewed as random and not associated with a factual event.

So, I assure you, the two or three hours of research is worth the time and may save you much embarrassment later.

CHAPTER 17

Determining a Haunting

So, how do you determine if some thing or some place is haunted? Waverly Hills Sanatorium, located in Louisville, Kentucky, is said to be one of the most haunted places in the United States. It opened in 1910 as a hospital to treat those suffering from tuberculosis in a serious local outbreak that became an epidemic. The facility was expanded in the 1920s to accommodate more patients. It is estimated that thousands died there during the next two decades. Due to the introduction of effective treatments and antibiotics, the hospital was closed in 1961.

Waverly was popularized by the TV shows *Ghost Hunters* and *Ghost Adventures* and was featured on many other programs. The site is now a haunted tourist attraction visited by thousands every year. Other than the misery, illness, and death that occurred at Waverly on a daily basis, specific hauntings are attributed to the suicide of two nurses. One was reported to have hung herself in room 502, and the other reportedly jumped from 502's window. Urban legends also say a homeless man was murdered and used in a satanic ritual on the grounds.

The possible origins for hauntings at Waverly are extensive, and that is where you as the paranormal investigator come in. You will carefully comb through the evidence and narrow down the possibilities, do the research, isolate and identify the manifestations, and categorize their behavior. You will deal with truths. Even if those truths are simply the feelings you have when you put down your electronic equipment, stand in a spot and experience the things around you.

Identifying Hauntings

In my opinion, it appears there are essentially two things that can cause what is defined as a traditional haunting: (1) an event, or (2) an emotion—mainly an emotion. It could be that an event occurred at a location and somehow imprinted itself on that location; or, a person is so strongly impassioned about a topic, place, or event that they or a part of them remains. It is initially imperative that the paranormal investigator identifies what mechanism is the cause of the haunting. It will provide a better understanding of when and where the haunting will take place, will better prepare the investigator to observe and document the event, and will protect the scene and the investigators against external and unrelated paranormal influences. Solid dedication in this initial research will provide a firm foundation for conducting the investigation.

EXAMPLE: Paint Store Hanging—Rockdale, Texas

In Rockdale, Texas, where I grew up, the paint store on North Main Street was said to be haunted. There was an old man there who had been a paratrooper with the 82nd Airborne Division in World War II. A few friends and I used to go in the store and talk with him. It was one of the old-style buildings connected to the buildings adjacent to it, along the street. It was standard old architecture with minimum street width; however, the depth of the building made up for it. It was a two-story structure with a narrow staircase. Oftentimes the old man would stack crates of paint under the stairs to make a nice display of whatever paint was on sale. I went in a couple of times and he had an old painter's tarp hanging there, blocking the view of the underside of the staircase and paint display. I once asked him why it was there. Very seriously he paused, and then as if he came to a decision, he asked me if I really wanted to know. I pulled the tarp aside and looked back there. Stacks of paint cans and a large SALE sign. Nice and neat. I told him yes, I wanted to know. And the old man said, "Because I see him there." He nodded toward the tarp.

I was silent; I didn't know what he was talking about.

He said the man's name; I don't remember what it was. Then he said, "He hung himself there. From the steam pipe."

I looked behind the tarp again. I saw the pipe he was talking about. It was about 1-1/2 inch in diameter, coming out of the wall to the edge of the staircase, and it turned 90 degrees down, leading through the floor.

"He tied a granny-knot around his neck," he said, "and hung himself right there. Sometimes I can see him. Sometimes I hear him."

This paint store owner was a combat vet. This was a man who had told me and other kids stories about running from the shelling in Germany and shooting at German tanks with bazookas and how the explosives didn't even scratch the tanks' paint. This was a man, standing in front of me, eyes glazed with excessive water, telling me he sees a man hanging in his store. He hears a dead man walking in his store. I often wondered if I took his story out of context. I wonder if he meant, in his mind's eye, he could see the man hanging. Or in his mind's eye, he could hear his footsteps because they had worked together so long. But I think he meant what he said. I believe sometimes—sometimes, he could see him there.

The Causes of Hauntings

A haunting will have a cause. It is up to the investigator to work toward determining what it is. At this point, there has not been a definitive study to outline the exact events that result in hauntings, so it depends on whom you ask. The exact causes of hauntings are up for debate.

When my wife, Lynn, and I went to the Winchester Mansion, the first impression I got was, "This woman was crazy..." Now the question is, was she crazy trying to avoid a haunting or curse, or did a curse or haunting make her crazy? If you are not familiar with the Winchester Mystery House, it was the home of the widowed Sarah Winchester, heir to the William Wirt Winchester fortune. Yes, the guy who made the Winchester repeating rifle that won the West. It appears that after Sarah and William lost their infant daughter, Annie, Sarah fell into a deep depression. Fifteen years later, William died of consumption (TB). Soon after, she consulted a medium to help her understand her misfortune. (This was in 1881, and she was worth only about $20 million at that time—that equals about $483 million today—and that was before the creation of the IRS...) The medium told her that she and her family fortune were being haunted by the ghosts of American Indians, Civil

War soldiers, and others killed by the guns her husband manufactured. She even said Sarah's life was in danger. Sarah was distraught, but the medium recommended that she move west and build a great house for the spirits, and if the construction never ceased, she would be safe. So that is what she did. She traveled to the Santa Clara Valley and built this grand spectacle of a house. The mansion is seven stories tall, and reportedly contains 160 rooms, 2,000 doors, 10,000 windows, 47 staircases, 47 fireplaces, 13 bathrooms and six kitchens. The construction was continuous until her death.

In the Winchester case, the hauntings or curse were presumed by the medium to be caused by multiple homicides and attached to the Winchester name and fortune through physical items such as the guns that did the killing. This is a presumption that is conditionally rational and something an investigator looks for when starting their inquiry. All paranormal investigators should start by asking themselves, "Does the haunting have an initial cause?"

All in all, it was apparent that following the medium's advice was a good choice. Sarah was productive and lived a full life. She later died in her sleep at the age of 82.

Classifying the Causes

Homicide is obviously a very personal, tragic, and emotional crime. Therefore, a reasonable person would assume that murder would be a likely cause for a haunting. Death under great sadness or utter confusion would be other causes. While homicide seems to be a reasonable cause, it appears that more than 30 percent of hauntings reported in the Austin area are a result of suicide. It was the highest number of any causes of death related to hauntings. Austin is fortunate enough to have a very low homicide rate. However, because Austin has a very supportive mental health community, many social programs and houses the state mental hospital, it draws a high number of persons with emotional challenges and has the highest suicide rate of any city in Texas at about 14 per 100,000. But that is small compared to the Seattle Puget Sound area at 26 per 100,000. So, I believe it is unclear what types of incident influences a haunting. The causes seem to be a variety and correlates, at least in Austin, to manner of death: homicide, accident, suicide, or natural.

The following numbers are compiled from a random sampling of hauntings in the Austin area, as reported by Fiona Broome in her book, *The Ghosts of Austin*, and by such tour groups as Haunted ATX, Haunted Austin, and Austin Ghost Tours. These seven causes appear to be related to the reported hauntings based on their percentages:

Suicide and Acute Depression	29%
Accidental Death	24%
Child Death	17%
Civil War Fatalities	13%
Murder	12%
Long Term Illness	4%
Other/ Unknown	1%

Classifying Motivation

I took a critical look at the causes of hauntings and then drew on my psychology background to review the emotional states associated with the listed causes: (1) anger / hatred, (2) love, (3) devotion to duty or honor, and (4) confusion. When researching a paranormal event, if it appears to be human in nature, as an investigator, you should strive to understand the motivation of this soul. Here are the categories:

Fear, Anger and Hatred. These emotions appear to be related to persons wronged in their life, abused by their closest associates, and/ or murdered. According to paranormal sources, these types of emotional manifestations can be a danger to the investigative team and measures should be taken to ensure that no team members are alone on site. Reports of people being scratched, hit with objects, pushed, and held down are often reported when dealing with an emotionally unstable entity. Teams should think about how they are going to protect themselves and their equipment from attachment once they leave the site. Depending on individual beliefs, this may be done through religious prayer, a spell of protection, or spiritual assurance that the team is there to help no harass.

Examples of problematic investigation sites are mental hospitals and dungeons, which are reported to be some of the most haunted places on earth due to the horrific abuses suffered by the patients and prisoners.

The Case of Love. It is believed that love can also motivate the deceased to stay in the place where they were truly happy, or to remain near someone they love and yearn to protect. The ghost of The Bride of Charles Fort, Ireland is one such case. On his daughter's wedding night, the commander of the fort executed an officer he found sleeping at his post, only to realize it was the man his daughter had married that very day. In one account, the distraught commander threw himself from the fort's rampart. In another account, he shot himself. Either way, on discovering their fates, his daughter too jumped to her death. She is now seen by soldiers, workers and visitors, dressed in white and silently visiting the place where she found brief love.

Also, the legend of the wife of Vlad Tepes (Vlad the Impaler also known in the west as Dracula) is a suicide case and one of love. It is said that during the 1462 war she was surrounded at Poenari Castle (in present day Romania) by the Turkish army and had been told Vlad was killed in battle. Her deep sorrow and refusal to be captured by the invading legion compelled her to throw herself from the castle wall into the Arges River far below. Like many tragedies, she was incorrect about the fate of Vlad and killed herself for no reason. The castle was later liberated, and Vlad was devastated by the suicide of his wife; he never forgave the Turks.

I have been to Romania and up the 1480 steps to Poenari Castle; it is a magnificent feat of engineering. However, there is no way she threw herself into the river from the castle wall, unless she turned into a bat and flew all the way over there.

Devotion to Duty or Honor. When a person, such as someone in the military, develops strong feelings toward his obligation or his country's cause, after death he may feel the need to remain on duty until he is properly relieved, or the conflict is concluded. Sometimes this is related to love; however, I separated the two because love and honor are separate concepts.

State of Confusion. An entity's behavior indicates they do not know they are dead, or they are lost.

Homicide and Suicide. A considerable amount of research has been devoted to understanding both homicide and suicide. Homicide has a greater impact on the community than any other crime. It is defined as the killing of one human by another, justified or not. If not justified, in Texas, a homicide becomes manslaughter or murder. It is imperative that law enforcement handles the incident professionally and expeditiously.

While suicide is often a true tragedy, as in the case of Robin Williams, a man who was truly ill and could have been helped, it often goes under reported in the media. It is the 10th cause of death in the United States and oddly remains a taboo subject in most circles. Many ghost tours feature homicides and suicides, especially in Las Vegas. According to the National Association of County and City Health Officials, Las Vegas is the number one city in the United States for suicides and has been since 1990, averaging 34.5 suicides per 100,000.

It is unclear whether the hauntings resulting from murder or suicide originate from the carnal human interest that people have for murder, the intriguing nature of it, or the innate fear of it. Do the circumstances surrounding a murder cause people to look for phenomena, which they then find? Or, do phenomena surface to an unsuspecting person and then become attributed to the event? These are two questions that should be forever in the minds of paranormal investigators; does the chicken or the egg come first? In other words, did an unsuspecting person come into the area with no preconceived notions of the place being haunted and witness an apparition? Or, were they expecting to see an apparition because others have reported seeing one?

In some cases, these questions are answered when an aspiring business person buys a building known for a haunting, such as a bed & breakfast, bar, restaurant, or hotel, with the express purpose of advertising it as a haunted experience and making money from it. Whatever the case, your investigative methodology should remain consistent.

Ritual Crimes and Torture

It doesn't take a genius to surmise that if someone befell their fate in a ritualistic crime or through torture, they may be sufficiently motivated to stay around and haunt the people or places related to their murder. Most modern-day ritualistic crimes do not involve murder; they are more likely to involve drug abuse, sex, and animal abuse.

However, when law enforcement professionals in Texas are along the Mexican-United States border, and they encounter Santa Muerte objects, they know it could point to evidence of a narcotic cult. Santa Muerte is believed to be a female deity and folk saint in Mexican-American Catholicism. She is the personification of death and ensures the safe passage to the afterlife to her devotees. Santa Muerte objects are often in the form of statuary representing a skeleton in priest robes made of plaster. When mistaken for common "headshop" trinkets, law enforcement officers bypass possible key evidence that could lead to discovering ritualistic kidnappings, torture, and murder committed by gang members or cartels. These are not folktales; they are very real techniques that some narcotics gangs use to instill fear and compliance in the unarmed citizens of Mexico. According to Dr. Robert Bunker, consultant to the FBI's Behavioral Sciences Unit, such items provide insight into the spiritual orientation of suspects, arrestees, persons of interest, and potential victims of Santa Muerte-linked killings.

It is rare to come across ritualistic locations, but when law enforcement or paranormal investigators do, it is incumbent upon them to know their limits and back out if the environment contains things beyond their knowledge; be smart enough to know when you are in over your head. Like every gang, cults will have their telltale marks such as an altar containing blood, bones, burned plastic police figurines, black statuettes, and black candles. These will have different purposes than a rainbow statuette, and blue and bone candles.

An example of gangs using cult-like rituals is Los Zetas, one of Mexico's fiercest cartels. They consider Santa Muerte (Saint Death) their patron saint. In the U.S. vacation mecca of Cancun, Mexico in June 2010, investigators found the bodies of six tortured victims, three with their hearts cut out and with the letter "Z" carved into their abdomens, in a cave outside of the resort city. Presumably, the killers belonged to the Los Zetas Cartel, and the victims belonged to a rival gang.

During 2008 in Nuevo Laredo on the Texas border, Gulf Cartel enforcers, one of the oldest organized crime groups in Mexico captured Sinaloa Cartel members, took them to public Santa Muerte shrines, and executed them. Analysis by a U.S. law enforcement suggests that the perpetrators killed them as offerings to Santa Muerte.

Understanding the ritualistic nature of a homicide will help the paranormal investigator organize their inquiry and comprehend the intent behind the murder. This should lead to informed speculation about what forces are at work and what may have happened to the victim's soul to create or contribute to a paranormal event.

Cults

On November 18, 1978, I remember watching the CBS Evening News with Walter Cronkite and seeing the report from Guyana, South America of the mass murder-suicide of the members of the People's Temple. The organizers had used cyanide-laced punch to facilitate most of the deaths (this is where "don't drink the Kool-Aid" comes from), although harsher measures were used on some of the others who refused to cooperate. All in all, 918 Americans died that day at the hands of fanatic cult leader Jim Jones.

A cult is a cohesive social group defined by a system of religious-type devotions directed toward a person or thing. These are usually organizations, small in number, and are not readily accepted by the mainstream. Fanaticism is a key behavior in cults and many members end up committing murder and suicide. Some examples include: the 39 voluntary suicides of Heaven's Gate cult whose goals were to meet with a passing comet; the murders committed by the Manson Family cult to show devotion to Charles Manson; the murder suicides of 101 members of the Order of the Solar Temple; and the 800-plus murder-suicides committed by the African Restoration of the Ten Commandments of God cult as preparation for the impending apocalypse.

If, through your investigations, you find yourself involved in any way with a cult group, distance yourself, remain vigilant with your personal safety, and report the activity to local law enforcement.

Satanism

When I became a cop in 1986, the popular paranormal investigation was that of witches and demonology, which had confusing overlaps. At our pre-patrol briefings, called "show-ups," supervisors would pass on the important messages of the day and often remind officers to be aware of anything in particular that may indicate satanic occult activities. The interesting thing about the increased reporting of satanic activity was the fact that we were the ones increasing the number of reports, not the other way around. Now, whether or not these signs were there all along and went unreported or we began to see signs of ritualistic evidence and began reporting it, the crime statistics increased, which indicated that we had an occult problem. It begs the question, does the human condition open its future to self-fulfilling prophecy by educating itself on a topic and encouraging awareness?

The same rules with occultism apply to satanism. If your investigations bring you into contact with any satanic group, distance yourself, remain vigilant with your personal safety, and report the activity to local law enforcement.

Cause and Effect

When I first worked as an instructor in law enforcement, officers would incessantly complain that they were not trained well enough in hand-to-hand fighting techniques. In most police academies, officers receive one, maybe two, weeks of defensive tactics training, enough to have an overinflated sense of proficiency and get themselves into trouble.

Anyone who knows anything about law enforcement will know that one week of training is not going to help much. However, what these officers didn't consider is, if you spend time teaching a cop to fight, he will look for opportunities to test his skills, thus raising the excessive force claims against the department, resulting in a loss of time and money. This demonstrates cause and effect at its finest.

If you decide to conduct intoxicated driving check points in one area, most of the people stopped will have been at one of the bars in that area, resulting in a majority of the arrests related to a certain bar, making it look like they are over serving their customers. When in fact, they are a narrow sample from a much larger and widespread problem of DWI. And that is what the 1980s did to Satanism and occultism. Because of this transient fascination with cults in the media, occult-related crime reporting increased from patrol officers and, for a time, was considered a priority. These cases landed on the desks of competent detectives who quickly ferreted out the hoaxes, standard criminal mischiefs inadvertently identified as occultism, and teenage deviant behavior. In the early 1990s the satanic occult problem, or "Satanic Panic" as it was dubbed, faded from view. I have worked in law enforcement for over 28 years, and I have not personally had a single satanic occult case since 1989. However, I am speaking from my experience in central Texas. I cannot speak for the occurrences on the Mexico border.

Power of Suggestion

In the fall of 2006, researchers at London's Goldsmith College designed an experiment to test whether exposure to electromagnetic fields (EMF) and low frequency infrasound would induce an increase of perceived paranormal experience. So, the head of the Anomalistic Psychology Research Unit, Christopher French, built a haunted room to which a participant would enter and then be selectively bombarded with EMF and infrasound. Nearly three quarters of the participants reported having more than three unusual feelings. However, the only statistically significant relationship in subjects that reported this was they had previously scored high on a test designed to rate their predisposition to these feelings.

What this suggests, according to French, is that some people are wired in such a way that they see something that is objectively there, but others don't have the ability to see it. However, he thinks there is a simpler answer: people tend to do what they are told to do. If I ask you to pay attention to the shadows in a dark room, you will see definable shadows. If I ask you to find shapes in the clouds, you will find shapes. If I ask you to locate occult ritual sites, you will report sites. The Goldsmith study suggests that once you are aware of what you're supposed to pay attention to, you will.

For over 20 years, I have not worked a single occult case. Is it (1) because they are so rare, or (2) because they are so secretive? I vote one and two, and this is why. Several years ago, I worked a case involving several affluent citizens involved in ritualistic sexual deviance. This case became so convoluted due to their ability to hide evidence and influence other witnesses that the case was closed with no definitive outcome. When your victim and witnesses go silent, there is not much more you can do.

Be an Expert in What You Do

If you decide to investigate a suspected satanic organization, a ritual event, or the place where a ritual event occurred, understand you may face considerable opposition and be in direct danger of extortion, blackmail, assault, kidnapping, and even murder. True satanic occultists participate in ritually sacrificing animals, mutilating animals on an altar, grave robbing, and murder. They drain corpses of blood and are often linked to drug and pornographic rings engaged in sacrifices involving children. As a hobbyist, I suggest you conduct your investigation with the assistance of a professional such as clergy, a law enforcement official, or other professional investigator. Doing this will ensure someone in authority knows you are conducting this investigation and is always aware of your whereabouts, law enforcement will not assist in your investigation unless there is reasonable suspicion that a crime has occurred; therefore, you will be on your own. Remember, occultists are ruthless, masters of manipulative psychology, well-funded, and ultimately dangerous. An occult investigation is not something you do for fun.

If you are interested in further research into the occult, I would recommend reading Kahaner's *Cults That Kill: Probing the Underworld of Occult Crime.*

The Mystery

It is my belief that the cause of a haunting is as individual as the people themselves. Each and every person behaves in similar but different ways. Each of us has our own ideas of the world and each of us is affected by people, places, and events in different ways. While I have outlined several factors that I think cause hauntings, there are obviously many other factors that could contribute.

CHAPTER 18
Classifying Sightings Events

The sexy part of the FBI is the profiler. The profiler is what TV programs portray as the backbone of the Behavioral Analysis Unit (BAU) of the FBI. Many movies and TV shows make it look like the profilers investigate all the intriguing cases and solve the unsolvable crimes with their supernatural intuition and psychological mastery, when, in fact, they do not.

Complex criminal cases are solved through rigorous, basic investigative techniques and resolute detective work. While the 10 to 20 profilers who work in the BAU do provide generalities that would point toward a certain type of person who may be prone to committing a certain type of crime, they are not the intuitive magicians portrayed by Hollywood. Just look at the DC Beltway Sniper case where 10 ordinary people were murdered at long distance with a rifle. Completely randomly, walking on the street, pumping gas, shopping, going to school, and a bus driver getting ready for his route. The suspects turned out to be the opposite of what the FBI profilers expected. Profilers predicted an educated white male, possibly military trained, driving a van. They had even said, this is something white males do. What they finally discovered was the DC Beltway Sniper was two black male transients driving a sedan. Profilers could not have been more wrong.

Profiling the Entity

One of the leading experts in paranormal profiling is Rosemary Ellen Guiley. She has an impressive amount of experience in dealing with any number of entities and has written extensively on isolating and identifying forces behind emergent phenomena. Her study into what I call Entity Behavior Identification

(EBI) has provided different evaluative perspectives when attempting to classify paranormal events and identify their causes. Often times we equate events to our own limited paranormal understanding. This leads to a misidentification of the entity or event and directs the experiencer down the wrong path. Using EBI, the observer categorizes the event using the five senses and a described emotion:

> **Sight:** Shape / Color / Intensity / Luminescence
> **Feel:** Environment / Tactile / Temperature
> **Taste:** Good / Bad / Specific
> **Smell:** Good / Bad / Specific
> **Hear:** Intensity / Recordability / Clarity
> **Emotion:** Good / Bad / Evil / Presence / Being watched

Once recorded, the investigator can categorize the observations and look for common occurrences that point toward a particular cause. Unless the phenomena change every time from case to case, this method will help to differentiate the ghost from the time traveler, the ET from the shadow person.

Apparitions. These entities or events can be classified in many ways. Frequently, an apparition is a "ghost-like" vision of something or someone. These can be determined to be hauntings, religious experiences such as the appearance of the Virgin Mary, an extraterrestrial encounter, or any number of other anomalous sightings.

Establishing proof: In theory, apparitions should be able to be captured on audio, video, or with a still camera. There is a debate among investigators as to the effectiveness of digital recorders and cameras versus old-school analog tape and film equipment. A well-rounded investigator should try to experiment with both.

Residual Hauntings. Residual hauntings are said to be energetic imprints left over from an event, such as wet foots prints that appear across a wooden floor then disappear, or the sighting of a ghost ship, train, or wagon traveling along the same path over and over. I had one young woman in Lee County, Texas tell me that as she walked in a wooded area along the family farm's back grazing pasture, she saw an American Indian sitting at an outcropping of rocks. He never looked at her but simply stared ahead as if he were watching something. As she got closer, he slowly faded. She called the vision a ghost. From an investigator's point of view, it could also be interpreted as a psychic impression, an event so momentous in the person's life experience that it is somehow burned into time and place. She said she saw it twice more before she graduated school and moved. Each time was the same.

Residual hauntings are like watching a movie, they do not change. And if you believe there is a human spirit involved, it is not conscious of its surroundings and does not deviate from its behavior. It repeats itself over and over until the event is disrupted by human involvement or over time simply fades away.

Some ghost tales speak of inanimate objects related to an event. These objects clearly do not have a spirit, so common sense would lead a reasonable person to believe something else is at work here. Such things could be imprints and burns, or psychic echoes of past events, or some sort of energy residue left behind. Whatever it is, it is something we have yet to understand.

Establishing proof: In theory, anything you see can be captured on video or film.

Interdimensional Visitors. It seems the science community's understanding of our world is expanding at a very rapid pace. Every year, there are more and more theories about the creation of the universe and how humans fit in. Many astrophysicists subscribe to the multiple universes or "many worlds" theory because it is the only explanation why many math calculations do not work as they should. These deviations lead them to believe there are "other forces" influencing our physical world that we cannot see and have yet to identify. Some of these are quantum theory, the identification of dark matter, multiple universe theory, and the Higgs Boson (particle).

The Higgs particle was found in March 2013 by smashing a lot of atomic particles together using the Large Hadron Collider (LHC) in Switzerland. In that process, some of the particles were slowed down by what is called the Higgs field, and in doing so that energy was not destroyed but gained mass created from Einstein's equation, E=mc2. Simply put, mass in motion is equal to a large amount of energy. Why would a ghost hunter need to know this, you ask? Because the Higgs particle obeys the conservation of energy law, which states that no energy is created or destroyed, but instead it is transferred. Could it be possible that inter-dimensional theory works in much the same way? Energies from one dimension somehow influence another or escape altogether into another? This theory of moving on to another plane of existence through death to an afterlife is as old as recorded history. The Higgs particle's behavior seems to support this transfer of energy theory. The possibility of multiple dimensions existing at the same time and in the same space would certainly explain mathematical influences we cannot otherwise see or account for.

Whether visitations are in the form of hauntings, UFO experiences, or religious in nature, the Interdimensional Visitation Hypothesis (IVH) should be considered in establishing the origin of such events. Many believe the IVH theory explains the vast distant problems with ufology travel, and that they are merely traveling from one dimension to another.

Time Travel Theory. There are many that believe the utter vastness of space prohibits any space travel to contact other worlds. In their minds, the distances that must be covered are simply too great for any kind of conventional transport. Even reaching the speed of light would require years, if not hundreds of years, to reach other habitable planets. To defeat these distances, and to explain what appears to be other worldly visitations, some believe the answer is time travel. Thus, visitations such as those described by extraterrestrial abductees are events created by Earth-bound future time travelers reaching back in their own history. They often equate shadow people experiences with the same explanation. While the true quantum mechanics have limited support in this area, the possibility cannot be discounted.

Shadow People. Shadow people are often interpreted differently by scholars of different schools of thought: religious, as demons or Djinn; Ufologist, as extraterrestrials; ghost hunters, as spiritual hauntings; police officers, as burglars. The truth is, no one can definitively explain what they are or what causes someone to witness the appearance of shadow people.

Shadow people experiences can result in unimaginable fear and anxiety for the experiencer. When dealing with people who have had these experiences, it is important to determine if the person has had the experience more than once and in multiple locations. If multiple locations are involved, this means the shadow person is following the experiencer around and observing them, or the person is experiencing multiple emotional disturbances, possibly due to a physical condition or post-traumatic stress. You must always be clear about the plausible causes first, then switch to the paranormal.

Demonic Possession. In the United States, according to a 2007 Pew Research survey 68 percent of Americans agree that angels and demons are active in the world. In a 2012 Public Policy Polling survey it showed that most people between the ages of 18 to 29 believe in direct demonic possession. While all of this may be true, polls also indicate those people that describe themselves as religiously affiliated has shrunk from 83 to 77 percent in 2014. Bottom line, the with population growth, human's belief in the supernatural is growing.

Law enforcement mental health or crisis units are charged with investigating persons reported to be experiencing or claiming to be possessed. I have investigated many acute mentally ill patients who have the signs and symptoms of both schizophrenia and demonic possession. Law enforcement does not handle possession; all behavior in such cases will be classified as socially unacceptable or criminal. The socially unacceptable will be diverted to psychologists for evaluation, and the criminal will go to jail. It is rare for law enforcement officials to do anything different.

In some possession cases, the person being possessed suffers very mild physiological or behavioral changes, and in others the perceived influence is dramatically pronounced. A person suffering from what they believe is demonic possession should first be cleared by a medical doctor. In some cases, physical conditions can produce signs and symptoms of what some consider demonic manifestations: catatonia, inappropriate emotional outbursts, aggression, and hallucinations. All of these can indicate a particular disease of the mind or a physical disruption such as brain injury or abnormality. Remember, you always investigate the most plausible explanation in an event and rule out naturally occurring phenomena before looking for the paranormal explanation.

EXAMPLE: The Charlatan—Rockdale, Texas

In 1981, and after my cow church scratching experience, I went through a transient religious phase. I had a friend of mine and a friend of my sister speak at length with me about God and religion; both were of the Charismatic faith but professed to be "non-denominational." They said they were not religious in the sense of being a part of a religion but simply believed in the Word of God.

I know...semantics...

Anyway, being raised Catholic, being a former altar boy, and having spent several junior high summer camps at the seminary in Houston, I had a little more knowledge about religion than the average person, at least in reference to the Catholic faith. I had attended several Sunday services there in Rockdale, Texas with my Charismatic friends and for the most part enjoyed the camaraderie of the congregation and the messages from the pulpit. Several times, I have to say, I was quite uncomfortable when the preacher professed in the open altar call, that God was telling him there was a very special young person among the congregation who was looking for absolution and to be saved. Silence would permeate the room and he would repeat himself, purposefully looking my way and nodding.

Now, I am certain that my friend and some of the other adults were telling the preacher to call me out; however, maybe that is the way the preacher defined that God was talking to him. Maybe that was his perception of how God works. I took it that he was saying God spoke to him about me, and that's how I was saved. One Sunday, the preacher finally called out my name to come forward and be saved. I did what I was told. I was hugged, congratulated, and told my new life begins now. The same thing others told me when I was confirmed in the Catholic Church, my new life begins now, began now... Here is the real problem: I knew then that sooner or later, they were going to get me up there to lay hands on me and I would have to fall down and be healed. This concerned me greatly.

A few more weeks went by and several of the Charismatic churches had a good old-fashioned tent revival and invited in a "real" man of God, a fire and brimstone preacher. Everyone who was "not religious" came to see him. The worship started with singing and music, then it led to a light version of "Sinners in the Hands of an Angry God," reminiscent of the long-deceased Jonathan Edwards. Halfway through his impassioned and intense admonishment of the gathered sinners, he paused, and then became silent.

Suddenly, his eyes bulged, his mouth opened, and he went into one of the finest impersonations of Fred Sanford's, "Elizabeth, I'm coming to join you, honey!" imitation heart attacks I have ever seen, before or since. I was in the third row and witnessed it all. He stumbled forward and hit the podium, stumbled back and bumped into the wall of the tent, which conveniently held him up, then forward down onto the floor, his hands leaving his chest for a brief moment to lessen the impact. And there he lay, between the podium and some folding chairs.

Several of the congregation went to his aid while several others stood and implored those gathered to remain in their seats. Others called for someone to call an ambulance (this was before 911), while still others told the congregation to call on the Holy Spirit to release their fallen brother from the demon that had taken hold of his heart and was crushing the life force from it. Yelps and wails of forceful demon commands came from the audience, and a rolling cacophony of speaking in tongues inflated the tent. Worshipers with eyes to the ceiling, eyes closed, and eyes covered by their hands, cried, and demanded their faith be revealed.

I watched as this modern preacher opened his eyes, elbowed the chair away from pressing against his ribs, and made himself more comfortable. He made eye contact with me for a split second then immediately feigned unconsciousness again. No one during a massive heart attack, adjusts his body for comfort and then lay motionless. I know this as a trained Emergency Medical Technician and now most certainly as a cop that has had numerous people fake medical conditions and fainting trying to get out of a trip to jail. They certainly don't fall to the ground and conveniently have their head land precisely on their biceps and not roll off. I instinctively knew that when I was a teenager. I had caught him in his lie and did not ignore his ruse like the others in the congregation. As true believers, they did not question his heart attack. I was the work of the devil.

After the summoned holy ghost drove away the demon that had meant to kill the preacher, and after he rose, shook the demon off and finished his sermon, he looked at me several times, but he never spoke to me again. Later that day after the service, he consumed two hearty plates of brisket, potato salad and baked beans before he left. Then the congregation left. All that remained were the plastic bags filled with discarded paper plates and plastic cups.

Thirty years later, while sitting in a barbecue restaurant, I scribbled this on a napkin:

The Charlatan

Of the bright signs—of the Bold and the red
Of the promised chatter—And of the things that they said.
The grown-up smiles and dynamic prayer styles
Of these things the child beguiles:
And files.
The morning comes—Yellow Sun and promise
White collars and ties—Congregation and solace.
It is the Elder's dream, with paradise abeam
The ancient creation they deem:
Or so it may seem.
I wonder upon—what is his fate
Excitedly, he smiles—Passing the offering plate.
Spirit smitten sinners, opossumed where they lay
It was then and there, the child walked away:
A Charlatan, he say.

Had I missed it? Had I missed the entire meaning of this possession event, this calling upon angels, this divining act? Were there people whose faith is so strong that the little deceptive clues to this staged medical miracle do not and would not matter? Am I missing the whole intent of this experience?

Was the purpose of these antics to reenact the times that demons did swoop down and crush man? Was that the lesson? Was there a need for theatrics to establish the fear and foreboding the people of the Bible felt every day? But, for good or bad, all I knew is that this man had lied to me. He had faked having a heart attack. And if he could fake a heart attack, he could fake speaking in tongues. If this was the case, maybe it was all a lie.

I knew then as well as today; lies destroy trust.

And I would not be tricked again.

CHAPTER 19
Close Encounters

It seems we all know someone with a UFO story—it is completely understandable considering how many flying objects traverse our skies every day. In 2017, according to the International Air Transportation Association (IATA), there were 36.8 million commercial air flights worldwide. The United States Federal Aviation Administration (FAA) reported as of 2018 there were more than 43,000 flights over the United States on an average day. This includes commercial flights, general aviation fixed wing flights, helicopter flights, and 5,200 military flights. In addition, in 2017 the Goddard Space Flight Center reports, that there are 2,271 manmade satellites in orbit; some are stationary and some travel about 17,000 miles per hour. All those numbers combined provides for some amazing statistics for misinterpreted aircraft.

The chances of seeing something you cannot identify in the sky is on the high side. The serious challenge with any UFO investigation is that the witness saw something in the sky that either looked or performed in an extraordinary way and is no longer there. The only thing you have to go on is their word of what they saw.

Many Witnesses

I have police officers, multimillionaires, private business owners, nurses, and a whole host of other professionals who have told me about their UFO experiences. The ones that throw me are reported by licensed professionals who know their credibility is at stake when they speak about it. I sat down with a high school teacher one afternoon and we discussed her experience. We will call her The Teacher. At the time of our interview, she was a 50-year-old biology teacher at a suburban high school. According to her, she had never been diagnosed with mental illness or epilepsy, had never taken hallucinogenic drugs or reported seeing visions. She was an average daughter, wife, mom, teacher, and homemaker. She lived with her husband and two teenage daughters in an 1,800 square foot, single story, wood and masonry single-family house, with a backyard and a chain-link fence. They had just over four acres and her nearest neighbor's house was about 300 yards away. She was in a semi-rural area, at least two miles outside the city limits near what was then Bergstrom Air Force Base, now the Austin-Bergstrom International Airport. One afternoon she heard her dog barking and "felt" something. She said she could not describe it except as a feeling that something was "correct," that she understood everything. It was a moment of clarity for her.

In my journey of paying attention, I have interviewed a total of four people who describe their experience this way, that everything seems to be "right," "in-line," or some sort of fleeting moment of lucidity. She moved the vertical blinds to the left of the sliding glass door, opened the door and then stepped through. In that moment, everything was blinding white and every sound was silenced. She described it like she was immediately submerged in water and silence overtook the world. She said she put her hand to her face, sheltering her eyes, and her back yard slowly came out of the whiteness. She said the light was as bright as staring into the sun. She peered up and saw the bottom of a huge metallic, disc-shaped object. As her eyes adjusted, it became clearer—then it was gone. Her back yard was normal, and she was standing on the porch. The sliding glass door was closed, and her dog was inside. She told me she had never told anyone about this, and that she would never tell anyone about this in public.

Like the others, I tried to talk The Teacher into making a report to the Mutual UFO Network (MUFON). I knew there was no reason to report it to law enforcement; they would simply send a mental health officer, like me, to evaluate her. Since then, she has lived in silence with her experience. It is in cases such as this that there seems to be a bit more credibility than in the multiple incidents reported by the chronically paranoid, or a bored person with histrionic personality disorder. Still, one can speculate any number of motivational reasons a person in a "normal" life may want to entertain an unusual experience.

The Teacher's account is the same as reported by others, an almost out-of-body event. When I went over her story, she remained consistent; after all, there was not much to report. It was so short. I broke the event down to core facts so we could dissect each: (1) hearing a dog barking, (2) moving aside the blinds and sliding open the glass door, (3) stepping out, (4) standing in a blinding whiteout, (5) seeing the object in the sky, (6) everything back to normal, with (7) the door shut, and (8) the dog is inside. She agreed that this is what happened. I asked the obvious question: how did the dog get inside? Like so many other seemingly irrational stories, she rationalized that he must have been inside the whole time. Then I asked who shut the door. She said she did, she thought... I asked her if she remembered closing the door, and she said maybe, then she said no. I asked who was in the house when this happened who could support her claim of this event. She answered, no one. Then I asked her again who was in the house. She thought, then changed her mind and said her daughter was home, but she was in the kitchen; they were getting ready to make dinner. I asked if the kitchen was near the sliding glass door and she said, yes, on the other side of the breakfast area. I asked if her daughter saw her go outside and she said she didn't know. She went on and said that when she came back inside, she sat down with her daughter and ate supper. I asked what she ate and she didn't remember. I asked her if they were about to make dinner and she walked outside for a brief minute, how the dinner could be ready when she came back in. She said she didn't know; maybe she was in the back yard longer than she remembered. Abduction experts would say maybe she was "somewhere" longer than she remembered, but it wasn't in the backyard.

In the case of The Teacher, we didn't have the opportunity to explore the event further. We were not in a place where I could do a regression interview, and we didn't have time to get a written statement so I could analyze and identify these missing elements. In a case such this one, or in a case involving the interview of a suspect, the truth often lies in what is missing, not in what is told. In my attempt to get more information, The Teacher did not advance her story. It seemed that everything she told me was everything she wanted to tell me or needed to tell someone. It seemed to me that whatever had happened, it had disturbed her, but she was content to not examine it further. At the time of our ad hoc interview, I was in my mid-twenties and knew very little about UFO reporting or abduction experiences. However, later in life, I would understand that it is common for some experiencers to accept what they had seen, yet suppress any desire to do anything about it, whether that be seeking out UFO experts or checking their mental status.

During The Teacher interview, it was obvious that the story she told was missing some elements of the event. The three real questions remain: (1) who put the dog inside? (2) who closed the door? (3) how did her daughter prepare their meal so quickly? There may have been completely rational explanations for these three inconsistencies; however, at this point, we will never know.

UFO Under-Reporting

In most UFO cases, the witness never reports the event. They take the experience as something unusual or unexplainable but shrug their shoulders and move on. These are the types of nondescript sightings that do not elevate the witness's imagination further: A light behaving strangely or changing colors in the sky. A light streak across the sky possibly attributed to a meteor. A misidentified satellite.

Events that should be reported are those that strike the witness as unimaginable or unexplainable. However, due to the stigma of those who report the sighting of a UFO, many experiencers decide to keep it to themselves and never divulge the event to anyone or only to a select few.

According to MUFON and other UFO research organizations, as many as 70,000 UFO sightings are reported every year. Researchers estimate that double or triple that amount that are truly witnessed. If you are not a member of MUFON or a similar UFO data collection organization, refer UFO witnesses to one of these groups. If you feel the person will not follow through, contact someone at MUFON and guide the witness to them. If that fails, ask the witness to write a statement for you. This statement can later be analyzed to clarify the event and it provides a baseline of what happened. If that also fails, at the very least, interview them as I did The Teacher and document their experience yourself. Here is where your skills as a professional interviewer come in. I have worked with cops who have never been to a single interview school, but out of pure instinct, intuition, and a self-understanding of deception, conduct the best interviews I have ever seen. Other cops, who have been to numerous interview and interrogation schools, could not even get an Eagle Scout to confess. You have to trust yourself and feel for the right questions. Once you conclude your interview with the witness, make the report yourself to MUFON; however, keep the confidentiality of your witness.

UFO Abductions

Every year, hundreds of people claim to be abducted by aliens. Most describe the grays who have large heads and black eyes, and project menacing mind control. My experience with UFO alien abduction comes from two places: my worked as a mental health officer, and acquaintances who found out I have been researching the Roswell Incident for over 15 years. As far as the mental health side, I interviewed and transported dozens of people to the Austin State Hospital suffering from what my technician-minded method identified as auditory and visual hallucinations. Now, many of these people had long histories of mental illness, long histories of drug abuse and prescribed psychotropic medications.

Whenever I received a call, I responded to the location, interviewed the experiencer, correlated their signs and symptoms to manifestation described in the Diagnostic and Statistical Manual (DSM), and either committed them to a hospital or released them. That was Greg, the technician. Greg, the detective, should have attempted to correlate the experiencer's story or, at least, establish a timeline of witnesses and places to verify that it was impossible for them to have been abducted.

The problem with the mental health community is the assumption that abductees are crazy. No mental health officer tries to establish a timeline; if you say you have been abducted and have a story, you are transported somewhere to be evaluated. It is a simple solution and part of professional case management. If you have been taught that something is completely impossible, there is no reason to try to prove it. Along the same lines, how do you prove missing time? The claim of alien abduction is possibly the most perplexing of all paranormal investigations. There are elusive excuses for every question. You should strive to eliminate all of the probable causes for someone experiencing what they believe is an alien abduction. Eliminate the possibilities of:

> Drug-Induced Psychosis
> Alcoholism
> Mental Illness
> Epilepsy
> Poisoning
> Head Injuries
> Lack of Sleep
> Prescription Medications
> High Fever
> AIDS
> Brain Cancer/Tumor/Cyst/Abnormality

These and other situations and conditions can cause the following hallucinations:

> Visual - eye
> Auditory - ear
> Olfactory - nose
> Tactile - skin

Unfortunately, these seem to be the most likely causes of abduction experiences. You must eliminate these possibilities before you decide to go on with the investigation. In Craig Glenday's work, *The UFO Investigator's Handbook,* he provides several examples of audacious claims by reported experiencers. In one 1954 case, Dr. Daniel Fry reported to have been invited onboard a UFO in the White Sands desert. He was told that thousands of years ago, a race of superhumans fled to Mars and were now re-establishing contact. We now know Mars is most likely uninhabited and the good doctor's report was either a delusion or a hoax.

Eliminating the Normal and Expected

When dealing with the extraterrestrial paranormal experience, the investigator must first eliminate the normal, physical, and mental causes. Whatever signs and symptoms left over are the potential paranormal ones. If an experiencer is not willing to do so, and simply wants to first concentrate on the paranormal event, the investigator may be completely wasting their time. Obviously, extraordinary events can cause strong emotions and post-traumatic stress, and even result in paranoia. It is understandable that a person who was abducted by aliens, subjected to tortuous physical experiments, and lost time, may ultimately suffer from mental disorders.

In turn, the investigator has to establish if the person was suffering from mental illness prior to any of their reports of abduction. Usually, people diagnosed with schizophrenia begin with delusions of small conspiracy theories, items mysteriously missing, then go on to their family watching them, the government surveillance of their home and person, micro-robots following them, and tales of abduction. If your witness has this sort of history, just remember, it could all be in their head. But then again, maybe the abduction event spanned many years and as a consequence they developed schizophrenia. This is where case management comes in. Ask yourself if pursuing this person's claims is worth your time and effort.

EXAMPLE: The Coworker

When I was 16 years old, I was the assistant manager of a restaurant chain. I had been a waiter for three months, and then a cook for six months. During that time, I asked the manager if I could learn what the assistant did. She agreed, and when the assistant quit, I was the only person who knew the job. One night, I was standing in the kitchen area reading a meal ticket as one of the wait staff walked up and stood directly in front of me. She stared unblinking with her mouth slack, and said, "They're here." Then she began to urinate. I heard it and saw her pants get wet with urine running down her leg. I grabbed her hand and tried to get her to follow me to the back of the restaurant, but she wouldn't move and became very stiff. I looked at her and said something like, "Come on, come back here." She just stared past me. At this point, the cook noticed what was going on and he tried to help, but she wouldn't budge. After possibly one or two minutes, her muscles slowly began to relax, and she became semi-conscious and able to walk. I took her to the back employee break table and sat her down. We called a family member who came to pick her up.

It wasn't until several days later that I was able to speak with her about the incident. (Remember in 1980, there were no cell phones or email.) She and I stood out by the loading doors and talked as she smoked a cigarette. She explained that this sort of thing had been happening all her life. It begins with very bright lights. If she is outside, they shine down like cones from streetlights; if inside, they usually shine through windows or cracks in doors or gaps in curtains. Everything around her stops and that's when it happens. She is taken from her body, put through immense torture and then returned. She was crying now. Not boo-hoo crying, or anger crying, but crying because these events have gone on for so long, and she knows they will continue. Crying, because she did not know how much longer she could take it. She said that years ago her mother took her to a doctor. The doctor said she had a scar on her brain, diagnosed her with epilepsy and put her on medication. The medication was supposed to lessen the intensity of the seizures. She said the medication was no longer helping.

So, the questions are, (1) did the naturally occurring scar on her brain cause the seizures and visions? Or (2) did the multiple abductions and experiments she was subjected to create the scarring? And (3) was the doctor working to cure her, or (4) part of a government cover-up to hide the knowledge of alien presence? Alien abduction cases are rabbit holes few investigators ever return from. Once you start following clues, they are never ending.

The interesting thing is, since that time I have met three other people who have almost identical accounts of the "epileptic seizures." I spoke with a prominent businesswoman in the Central Texas area. Her experiences are much the same except she does not urinate and she has movement and free will. She sees the cones of light and can go outside to observe them. In one case, she went outside and observed dozens of these lights shining down from hovering objects in the sky. This occurred in the middle of the night over a small, incorporated city. She even woke her daughter; however, the lights were gone before her daughter could get outside. There were no reports of this event from the residents of the town.

Here is where the problem occurs. When I asked her about getting a CT scan, MRI, or other medical procedures to rule out a physical condition, she declined. I even explained that the scans should reveal any implants, but she was still uninterested in anything other than the paranormal event. This of course is where my assumptions and expectations influence my investigation. If the competent person does not wish to conduct a methodical and proficient investigation, they are not truly interested in learning the facts about their experience.

In most cases, establishing cause is impossible without the witness's cooperation. If so, such cases go unsolved or undetermined. However, that does not mean we cannot later use the information gleaned from the investigation to support credibility of another case.

CHAPTER 20
Cryptids

No paranormal investigation book can ignore the search for the elusive cryptids of the world. While I have spent much time in the wilds of Texas, California, Washington, Alaska, North Carolina, Central America, and Egypt, I do not have an informed background in cryptozoology. However, I do have a good understanding of biology and the identification of evidence associated with animal movement and behavior. This provides me a foundation from which to review the possibilities of unclassified animal existence and the likelihood of their existence. For example, in such cases as the Loch Ness Monster, one can calculate the size of an animal and the animal's environment in reference to the environment's ability to support that animal. As for Nessie, there is not enough food in the loch to support an animal of that size. Therefore, based on contemporary knowledge, the likelihood of Nessie's existence is in doubt.

Conventional zoology considers cryptozoology to be pseudoscience. These zoologists often ignore the possibilities of cryptid existence because often the claims made by cryptozoologists do not have enough evidence to support the animal's existence. This is because, in most cases, there is no physical evidence, just a sighting or an experience. Moreover, where there is evidence, very few are willing to fork over the money for legitimate material testing; and nowadays, DNA typing is inexpensive. So, that tells me there is very little biological material gathered from cryptozoologists to be tested.

In my law enforcement career, I cannot tell you how many deer I have had to put down because they were suffering after being hit by a car or getting hung at the top of fancy wrought iron fences. Early in the morning, I have seen groups of coyotes trotting down the sidewalks in the sprawling new, master-planned communities in western Travis County. I have seen a fox climb a six-foot tall chicken wire wall and wedge himself between the roof and the wall to drop in the coup, eat his fill, and then get trapped when he was too full of chickens to get back out. During the last drought, I saw deer lie flat on the ground and wriggle under chain link fencing to get onto a baseball field to eat the freshly watered grass. Animals, when threatened, or forced into a situation, can do amazing things. Why should we be surprised that a species has evolved to hide from man at all costs? After all, some ignorant humans kill everything they see. I would try to avoid humans too.

In 2014, there were 1,400 new animal types added to the World Registry of Marine Species, and many new land species were discovered to include cartwheeling spiders, the world's second longest insect (a newly discovered walking stick), a beaked whale, and a carnivorous mouse—my favorite. However, the Earth is losing far more animal species at an alarming rate due to pesticides, pollution, and human expansion into their native habitats. It is expected that in the next 100 years, the Sumatran rhino will be gone due to poaching, lowland gorillas will go extinct because of poaching, monk seals due to pollution and fishing gear, vaquita porpoises due to gill nets, pangolins from poaching and China's meat demand, and the Iberian lynx due to loss of habitat and declining food sources. These extinctions are a few examples of man's impact on his environment and the reason that many species are almost gone. The fewer the species, the more elusive, and the more widespread they are, the more likely they are to be determined a cryptid.

There are many cryptids that have been popularized by movies and television. Bigfoot, the Loch Ness Monster, and the Mothman have been big box office sellers. Some cryptids have been proven to be hoaxes or confirmed as innocently misidentified, such as the photographs of the flying "rods" or "skyfish" that previously flooded the Internet. These flying rods ended up being nothing more than normal bugs flying too fast for the low resolutions security to capture. They were viewed on video as long streaks of light with wavy fins on either side resembling some sort of unknown lifeform.

However, many cryptids that were thought to be mere legend have been discovered to be true. The tale of the Kraken, a giant squid that was said to attack sailing ships, was one of these. It was assumed a sea story until 1978 when the USS *Stein*, a U.S. Navy frigate that I sailed with during a western Pacific deployment, had its bow sonar dome damaged during at sea operations. Once back in port, it was inspected and found that 8% of the dome contained cuts in its thick rubber protective coating. These cuts contained remnants of very large claws, the same type of claws contained in squid suction cups on their tentacles. Based on their size, scientists estimate the squid would have to have been at least 150 feet long. In 2003 a French sailboat was attacked by a squid whose tentacles were said to be the thickness of an adult human's thigh. There is little doubt that many of the tales of sea monsters are now believed to be true.

According to Jeff Belanger, some of the most famous cryptids are certainly based on real animals, or animal-like creatures. Among them are the Bigfoot or Yeti-type creatures, chupacabras, The Loch Ness Monster, and any number of half-human, half-beast creatures such as the Goatman, Mothman, or werebeasts, like werewolves and werebears. In some cases, these cryptids are in only specific locations, like the Monster of Brey Road, the Skunk Ape of Florida, the Dover Demon, the Beast of Truro, the Lake Worth Monster, and the Fouke Monster, also known as the Legend of Boggy Creek. Many of the origins of the sightings are lost to time.

I am not a specialist in this field. However, in any of these cases, an investigation is an investigation. While it will help if you have a basic knowledge of biology and local animal species, an in-depth background in zoology is not needed. Gather your information, conduct your interviews, do your research, and plan your on-site operations. Who knows, one day you may help add a new species to the list.

However, if doing a cryptid investigation is out of your comfort zone, I suggest you locate and report your information to a cryptozoologist in your area. That's what I would do. For more information, I have included some excellent references in the bibliography.

PART FOUR
Scene Management

CHAPTER 21
Building the Team

For the past several years, I have been isolated from many employees where I work. On the rare occasion that I do see other deputies or corrections officers, they often say they miss having me as the firearms instructor and range master at the academy. Most ask if I miss it. My answer is no, for a whole host of reasons. However, my experience as the lead firearms instructor and curriculum developer at the range taught me a lot about myself and my fellow man.

Through this lesson I learned that there is nothing harder than standing in front of a group of your peers and trying to change the way they have always done things or change the way they have thought about things. With cops, you must be very careful; their egos are the biggest hurdle you face. Building a team with cops takes assertiveness, being a master at negotiations, and stamina. And believe it or not, it is not much different with a volunteer force; volunteers do not have to be there. The time they are donating is expensive to them. If you do not make them feel welcome and valued, they will eventually go away. Some you might even want to go away, however, when building a team, unless someone is truly destructive to the organization, they will have a purpose and provide valuable input.

You as a team leader must strive to identify that purpose.

Leadership

A team must have a leader, and a leader is not just the person who decides to start a team; they may start it, but they may not be suited for a leadership role.

EXAMPLE: SWAT Call Out—Central Texas

In 2002, I was assigned as a SWAT officer. One evening I received a page about a barricaded person, a possible hostage situation, at a local restaurant. As I lived very close to this location, I was one of the first SWAT personnel to arrive, and I assessed what I could see. Patrol cars were parked at all four corners of the building with officers pointing shotguns and covering the building exits. One of the deputies came over and identified himself as the incident commander. I assumed he was the senior person on scene. A few SWAT team members set up a staging area on the other side of an adjacent business. Several personnel were to deploy as a REACT Team (an ad hoc group of officers whose job it is to stage close to the incident and if violence erupts, to stop the violence through superior violence—sorry, but that is the way it is done). I was on that team, and we proceeded to the back door of the business. I had been in the building many times and the others with me knew the layout also. As we moved past the patrol unit covering the back door, I noticed the shift lieutenant kneeling beside his car with a shotgun resting over the hood. I thought to myself how derelict he was for not taking charge of the scene and being the incident commander. He had more time on the street than anyone, was senior in rank to everyone, and he was assigned to be the supervisor of the shift. He was also getting paid twice what the patrol deputies were getting paid! The whole situation bothered me.

However, I thought about this lieutenant's capacity of leadership; he had the training and ability to assess the situation and make an informed decision. In doing so, he made the decision to let someone else who could do it better take charge. Even though he had 25 years on the street, he had never been a SWAT officer or a negotiator; he was out of his element. Being the senior officer on scene, he was ultimately responsible for that scene. Did he show that he did not know the procedures, capabilities, and action plans currently in place for such situations? No. Should he know all the things SWAT knows and practices on a daily basis? Maybe. But, he didn't. He did, however, know how to solve the problem; he took himself out of the equation. He elected to assign a five-year, newly trained, field-training officer as the incident commander. Several hours later, the hostage was released, the suspect went to jail, and everyone went home uninjured.

Leadership is a desire, not a tactic. In most instances, you cannot educate people to be great leaders; you can give them generic leadership acronyms to use, management styles to imitate, and principles to emulate, but leadership is not a trait that is taught. Leadership is emergent; it will come forward when the time arises. When the football is dropped, do you want the ball? Do you immediately grab it and run, or do you think about it first? Do you wait to see what others will do? Leaders want the ball. They are not comfortable waiting and watching, and they are willing to take the chance and willing to make a mistake. Leaders understand that making mistakes is part of the learning process. If humans always did everything correctly, they would never learn anything. Leaders know this. Leaders recognize a person's strengths and can guide them into the assignment where they are best suited. This comes from a consultative or participative style of leadership. It does not mean every decision is made only after a discussion and a vote. It means that management welcomes ideas and input.

Roles and Responsibilities

When developing a new idea or facilitating change, you must create involvement and buy-in with those affected. Once they have buy-in, they have a vested interest in the success of the endeavor. This can make all the difference in the world when it comes to the legitimacy of the paranormal investigation. But, even then, personalities can muddle the mission and sometimes friendships. The interaction of engaged leaders is required to manage these relationships, identify points of contention and lessen the potential damage. Employees have buy-in—they are getting a paycheck. They have tangible reasons to put up with bad conditions, poor equipment, and lack of a clear objective or leadership focus; they are getting paid. In a paranormal team, leaders must recognize and address the issues. The price of not paying attention is low morale and a negative environment. As the department firearms range master, I supervised students, other assigned academy instructors and range assistants in everything from signing in students, to range supervision, to qualification scoring. It was commonplace that no matter how many times I would say it, instructors and assistants would allow themselves to stray from their assigned duties and be distracted with handling a problem that was the responsibility of another. In most cases, the industry standard ratio of instructors to students on a range is 1:7. While on the firing line, one instructor is responsible for the actions of up to seven students, and the less the better.

However, some people simply never get it. Inevitably, at least one of the instructors would see one of the other instructor's students do something and take it upon himself to assist or correct that student. It is a simple fact that if you are watching someone else's student, you are not watching your own. This degrades the effectiveness of your work and interferes with the function of the others. Do your job and the other issues will sooner or later fix themselves. If you do not think the person in charge is doing a good enough job managing the assignments, get more education for yourself, more training, and more experience and put yourself into a position where you can make the assignments and take the overall responsibility.

It is discouraging to see volunteer teammates go at each other's throats over power struggles. Trust me, if everyone simply does what is in their scope of responsibility, the evolution will smooth itself out. This is proven over and over through the study of Complex Adaptive Human Systems (CAHS). No matter the discipline, the human factors remain the same. These dynamics will manage themselves if everyone will do their assigned task.

Paranormal Organizational Structure

Traditionally, a chain of command is designed to allocate responsibilities and assignments to a manageable level within an organization. It also provides for an understandable matrix that everyone can comprehend to handle the flow of information and needed action. The chain of command has many different examples, and most are unique to the individual organization. Chains of command are typically structured in three parts: (1) Leadership— who is making the decisions, (2) Administration—who is coordinating behind the scenes, and (3) Technical—who is getting the job done.

Within paranormal investigations, a team should assign members' roles. Depending on the size of the team, certain team members may have more than one role. Teams should consider the following assignments: (1) Team Leader, (2) Assistant Team Leader, (3) Historian, (4) Researcher, (5) Record

Keeper, (6) On-Scene Technologist, (7) Assigned Investigators, (8) Advisors, (9) Logistical Support Specialist, (10) Team Medic, and (11) Safety Officer.

Team Leader. In charge of the mission of the organization and typically organizes events, assigns roles, plans strategies, and is responsible for the actions of members of the team.

Assistant Team Leader. As assigned by or in the absence of the team leader, is in charge of the mission of the organization and typically organizes events, assigns roles, plans strategies, and is responsible for the actions of members of the team.

Historian. The historian is often someone not directly related to the investigation itself who has detailed knowledge of the area or someone who has direct access to historical information about the area. The Austin Historical Society is an example of an organization to which one could go and discover historical public records about locations, properties and persons.

Researcher. The researcher is someone who has access to contemporary knowledge or information that would lead to a clearer understanding of the locations, properties, and persons. For instance, someone with the knowledge of how to search deeds or tax information on the building can identify previous ownership. The researcher can also be the historian and often is, yet they often use different means to discover information.

Scribe. The scribe is assigned to provide the written record of the investigation. The scribe should gather all paperwork obtained by the Historian/Researcher, and all other members of the team, and compile it into chronological order. They provide the final report and conclusion to the event. Any member can be the scribe; however, they must be highly organized, write well and be detail oriented.

On-Scene Technologist. A technologist is a highly sought-after member of your team. There are too many times where investigators show up at the scene ill prepared and lacking equipment—usually batteries. Having an on-scene technologist provides a problem-solving expert in all things technical and can save you unwanted downtime.

Assigned Investigators. Team members assigned to the needs of the investigation, usually by the team leader or assistant team leader.

Advisors. Persons with specialized knowledge of the area, the phenomena, the history, or anything else unusual that may require an expert.

Logistical Support Specialist. Some people want to be a part of the investigation but are not interested in being an investigator; they can still be very useful. Logistical support requires persons uniquely qualified to provide incident site setup, arrange delivery of equipment and other required materials, coordinate with other entities who provide services for the investigation, and provide directions and traffic control. This person also must have the ability to fix things, and to ensure food and water are available to the crew.

Team Medic. A person certified in first aid and CPR, who monitors the team members' physical conditions to ensure everyone remains safe in the investigation.

Safety Officer. A person experienced in identifying and minimizing hazards.

Reality Roles

As an example, if the Central Texas Paranormal Detectives (CTPD) has five members respond to an investigation, the team member breakdown of responsibilities may look like this:

> Member 1: Team Leader, Researcher, Assigned Investigator
> Member 2: Assistant Team Leader, Team Medic, Safety Officer
> Member 3: Assigned Investigator, On-scene Technologist
> Member 4: Assigned Investigator
> Member 5: Historian, Record Keeper, Logistical Support

In this example, there are no advisors assigned, but everyone knows whose job is whose. As long as everyone performs their duties, the investigation will flow and problems will be minimized.

Assigning roles will identify responsibility when something is not done and will simplify delegation. This will help keep the investigation running smoothly and efficiently.

Chapter 22
Managing Onsite Investigations

Managing investigations essentially has two parts: (1) the event itself, and (2) the persons investigating it. It is the administrative portion of the investigation that is difficult to manage; most competent investigators can break down the investigation into a series of tasks on a "to do" list and begin working the problem. Assigning responsibilities and tasks to members, ensuring those members complete those tasks, and ensuring the individual members are not interfering with the other members' duties is a never-ending cycle for team leaders.

To improve management of an investigation, supervisory members need to assess the lessons learned from other ghost hunting experiences. Ask a cop about the show *Cops* and he will tell you that it is a great show to learn what NOT to do. While that statement is not fair in all the cases, many of the actions taken in that show can be reviewed, and better choices can be gleaned for the next time you or someone else is faced with a similar situation. That can be done with a whole host of shows involving law enforcement, as well as ghost hunting. You cannot learn from doing things correctly. Identify what you have done wrong and formulate a better response for the next time you are faced with that similar situation. The smartest way to do this is not to make a bunch of mistakes; it is to learn from others who have already made those mistakes. Review ghosthunting shows and ask yourself, "How would I have done it?"

Using Investigative Outlines

Many people ask me how to conduct an investigation. Most people would like to see a matrix, or a series of steps so they can stay on track and check off the boxes to ensure nothing is missed. Many paranormal groups have created such lists. Many of these lists are just step-by-step charts of how to do the actual on-site investigation itself, such as this list of suggestions provided by http://examiner.com:

1. Meet at the location in the daylight and do a walk-through.
2. Set up your equipment.
3. Protect your team with a prayer or spiritual protection charm.
4. Walk through the area to see what reaction there is.
5. Start taking photos and asking questions.
6. Turn the lights on and pack up.
7. Say goodbye and thank the spirits for their time.
8. Once finished, review the evidence you collected.

This is a simplified list of how to conduct a ghost hunt. It advises nothing about the prior research of the phenomena, a witness on scene orientation, reconnaissance of the site, eliminating ambient influences, assigning roles, etc.

Now, it is obvious that as investigators, we do not want to be encumbered by a stack of rules and procedures that will dictate our every move. Flexibility is strength and rigidity is a weakness. However, it is helpful to have the general foundation of a directional guide that will keep all members on track, and one that will be agreeable to other reasonable people. The website http://www.wikihow.com suggests six steps that offer a more thoughtful process when conducting the investigation:

1. Look for a logical explanation.
2. Research your location.
3. Try to duplicate the experience.
4. Try to capture the experience in a different way.

5. Remain objective.
6. If you have a significant experience, call in the pros.

These two examples are at either ends of the spectrum as each is a generalization of what is entailed in researching a paranormal event. Each paranormal investigating organization will have its unique strengths and weaknesses. Therefore, their approach to the investigation will be different than other organizations. The challenge is: will or does the way you conduct your investigation pass a peer review? Will other investigators be able to look at your methods and processes and say, yes, that is a (1) reasonable way to gather research, (2) responsible way to conduct an investigation, and (3) sensible interpretation of the evidence accumulated.

WARNING: If you got your ghost story off the Internet, ran around the site threatening the ghost to quit hiding and show itself, and identified every orb and rod in your pictures as proof of a haunting, you will not receive a good peer review.

PACE Planning

One thing I got out of my experience in the Army that I continue to use to this very day is PACE Planning: Primary, Alternative, Contingency, and Emergency planning. Once you understand PACE, you can easily form a plan that is simple but comprehensive. For example, if you were making a plan to investigate a large structure and you are going to have multiple people in various areas at the same time, you may want to set a communication strategy:

> **Primary:** Everyone is on the handheld radios
> **Alternative:** Too much radio traffic, use a cell phone
> **Contingency:** No comms on radio or cell, send a text message
> **Emergency:** If nothing works, try yelling!

There can be a PACE Plan for everything you do. If a team member is injured, your PACE injury strategy can be:

Primary: Respond to and treat the person in place
Alternative: Walk the injured to the command post and treat
Contingency: Carry the injured to the command post and treat
Emergency: Call 911 and have first responders come to the scene

Obviously, you don't want to PACE an operation to death, but you will identify the truly important evolutions in your operations plan that will benefit from setting PACE.

Creating the Operational Plan

With the right understanding, anyone can create an investigative mission or operations plan. There are thousands of ways to do it. Remember, every team is different, so every ops plan will be distinctive. The plan will act as a guide for the team briefing, outlining the paranormal background, goals of the plan, personnel and equipment assignments. The following items are things to consider when making your operations plan:

1. Draft a brief description of the paranormal event
2. Draft a brief mission goal
3. Obtain the physical address of the site
4. Obtain the layout of the structure
5. Note hazards, steps and stairways
6. Identify active utilities, electric, water, and gas
7. Establish a command post
8. Establish an emergency medical triage area
9. Assign parking areas for vehicles
10. Assign a staging location(s) for personnel
11. Assign a staging location(s) for equipment
12. Assign personnel tasks
13. Assign an assembly point for the entry team to gather
14. Assign a single travel route to and from the entrance
15. Assign a single entry and exit point into the structure
16. Have an on-site sign-in/out log

While having a plan is necessary to limit confusion, accomplishing the goal is far more important than having a flawless operations plan. My suggestion is that you develop a form unique to you and your team, print several out, and then fill them out in pencil. This will allow you to easily make changes and reassignments. An operations plan is meant to be a helpful guide, not the law.

Don't Overlook the Potential for Emergencies

Presuming you have done all your research, interviewed persons with information, and decided to conduct a site assessment or walk-through, you should ensure you obtain relevant information for the operation plan. A site assessment is typically done during a walk-through. Some consider it to be the same thing; I do not. A site assessment can be done at the same time as a walk-through, but it is just a little more complex and geared toward ensuring that if there is an emergency on site, everyone is very familiar with not only the hazards but how to get themselves out. In the site assessment, you should gather the following additional information:

> **Hazards:** Note any potential hazards, mark if necessary
> **Layout:** Note or sketch the layout of the structure
> **Entry and Egress:** Identify doors, windows, and other openings
> **Physical Barriers:** Fences, perimeter walls, etc.

Hasty Plan

A hasty plan is exactly what it sounds like. It is most often used when time is limited, when a phenomenon suddenly presents itself, or when an unexpected opportunity arises. The smoothest approach to a hasty plan is:

1. Someone takes charge
2. A goal is identified
3. A quick review of the location and ways out
4. Personnel assignments are made
5. Time limits are set (if applicable)

6. Personnel performs their assignments

7. An after-action assembly point is designated

8. Re-assignments or debriefing

Mission Briefing

It is best if one designated person, preferably the one who prepared the operations plan, presents the briefing before beginning the operation. In some cases, the operations plan can be emailed to team members. One problem with this is someone may second-guess assignments or other organizational specifics and start a "fix the ops plan" email barrage creating unnecessary stress. If this is a possibility, just inform everyone where to park his or her cars and gather someplace close for the mission briefing.

The briefing should consist of reading the operations plan and making assignments. Once this is done, the presenter will quickly address every team member and ask them, "What is your assignment?" The person will then brief-back their understanding of what their assignment is and what responsibilities they have. If corrections need to be made, they will be made at that time, before moving on to the next team member's brief-back. Once completed, personnel are instructed to meet back at the staging area at a certain time to begin the investigation, or immediately instructed to begin their assignments.

If you follow this or a similar structure, everyone should be ready to go.

Actually, more than ready.

CHAPTER 23

Processing the Scene

On scene investigations can be the most fun and the most tedious part of the project. While you have accomplished locating the place, now you will decide what actions to take. There is no standardized list that you will follow every time. However, it is good to adopt a list of every possible task that could be taken at a scene and check off the ones you use. The main thing you are looking for is consistency in your investigative process, but sometimes you may have to veer off course and improvise; i.e., using gummy bears as movement detectors. Even though not scientifically proven, sometimes you have to work with what you've got.

Defining the Limits of the Scene

Through your exhaustive research, you will be able, and will need, to estimate the boundaries of your investigation. Otherwise, the entire world's phenomena are a part of your exploration, and everything is all piled together. There must be separation. In some cases, because of the change of the location, it is difficult to narrow down where it is likely that an event will occur.

When I was five years old, I remember my mother taking me to Capitol Plaza, a popular shopping center in Austin. We drove past a large horse farm on the west side of Interstate 35, near Highway 290. I thought it was cool because you could see the family graveyard; my mother, the master punster, told me people were just dying to get in there. At five, the reference went six feet over my head, or under. Either way, I didn't get it. But, anyway, several years passed and the first indoor mall was constructed on the site of that horse farm and atop that graveyard. Joske's Department Store sat right where those deteriorated gravestones had stood. Come to find out years later, when I worked at Joske's, it was said to be haunted. Many employees reported strange occurrences in the dock area. These were often reported as odd sounds and the feeling that someone was watching them. Personally, it always felt creepy to me to have to go into the warehouse dock area, but I could not place my finger on anything specific.

Trying to define the limits of your investigation and the limits of your haunting, or influence of your phenomena is an important reality. How far can the phenomena reach from its source, presuming there is a fixed point of reference? This is something you will have to determine on your own.

Urban Exploration

This is a lovely way of saying, "criminal trespassing." In Texas, criminal trespass is a Class B Misdemeanor, carrying a fine of up to $2,000 and up to 180 days in jail. Most urban explorers live by the words, "do no harm; leave no trace," so cases of criminal trespassing rarely come to light.

In 1985, I was assigned with the Multinational Force and Observers in the Sinai Desert, Egypt. At the time, we were under United Nations' command and conducting training exercises in conjunction with an Egyptian parachute regiment. During the day we often slept in small caves in the rock face, and at night we conducted operational patrols. I had several weekends off for rest and recreation (R&R) and tried to make the best of an existence in the desert. After being transported by helicopter across a demilitarized area where many of the armored vehicles from the 1973 Arab-Israeli War were still sitting either abandoned or destroyed, I and several others in my platoon decided to get some vehicles and go back to that area for some urban/desert exploration. Our lieutenant was maybe 24 years old and was easy to talk into going back and checking it out. After all, it's literally in bum-#$%&, Egypt—who would know?

Later that day, we acquired two large Mercedes trucks and headed out. Once there, we searched among the ruined Soviet tanks and trucks left rusting and half buried in the shifting sands. That's when we were first fired upon. Maybe five or 10 miles off, it's hard to tell in the desert, an Egyptian helicopter patrol spotted our dust trails and decided to give us two warning shots. That woke us up and we decided it was time to head back to camp.

Trespassing is not without its dangers. Urban exploration is simply described as the pure enjoyment of exploring places that most people wouldn't go. The experience of maneuvering mazes and obstacles of days gone by. The adrenaline rush of the unexpected. Finding footprints where you wouldn't expect them. This is urban exploring. And this is why we love it.

Be aware that if your ghost hunt is taking place on someone's property and you have not obtained permission to be there, you are "urban exploring," trespassing and can be arrested. You are trespassing because someone, a corporation, a trust, a company, or a government owns everything in the United States. Everything has some person or organization that exercises care, custody, and control over it. With condemned properties it is usually the city or the bank. In any case, law-abiding citizens request permission to enter such areas or buildings. However, the City of New York is never going to grant an "urban explorer" group permission to explore the old subway tunnels. Detroit is not going to allow urban explorers to wander through condemned manufacturing plants. Chicago is not going to grant entry into vacant tenement buildings. And Jim Bob the farmer is not going to let you explore the historical site of the Spanish Mission that is somewhere on his land.

Most likely, urban explorers will not be given permission to enter any property where misfortune could occur. If some sort of accident did arise, and someone had granted the group permission to be there, the grantor would be liable for any damage or injury. Therefore, most urban explorers don't ask for permission; if caught, they ask for forgiveness. If you find yourself facing such a decision and choose to forgo the law and take your chances, at the very least organize a comprehensive mission plan. Ensure you: (1) recon the area and determine multiple exit strategies, (2) assign as many lookouts as you need, (3) decide on effective communications, (4) use stealth, and (5) be slow and deliberate about your pursuit; do not rush into the unknown. Also, it would be best to already know a good bondsman and have enough money to post your bail, should Johnny Law outsmart you.

Being a Professional

If you want access to interesting areas that are normally off limits, and you want to do it legally, you must conduct yourself as a professional. Those who are permitted onto sites have the connections or the professional clout to support them. Professional photographers dedicated to their passion have websites, resumes, and connections that pave the way into places just like these. Hint, hint. Start small, get organized, and be serious if you are looking at becoming a professional urban explorer. Who knows what kind of ghost hunting you can do while you are there.

More information can be found at Urban Exploration Resource: www.UER.ca

First On-Scene

It is quite possible that the team member first on the scene will discover there has been a change to the scene or additional information is learned that will cause a change in the investigation. This information must be immediately shared with the lead investigator who can disseminate it to the rest of the team if they choose. Also, incorrect information can affect an investigation. Should you or your team receive misleading information, at the earliest possibility, brief the team and eliminate any subsequent influence from the investigation. If need be, adjustments to the operations plan can be addressed and corrected.

Walk-through / Site Assessment

The primary purpose of the walk-through of the location is to identify any dangers that would compromise the safety of the investigators and to familiarize the investigative team of the layout. The secondary purpose is to discover evidence. You are looking for any physical thing that will support the investigation. Marks in the structure (blood spatter), material from the incident (clothing), personal items of the departed, personal writings from anyone that advances the investigation, and any physical material related to the case.

The problem with the walk-through as a fact-finding mission is that it could potentially influence positively or negatively whatever phenomena might be present. It is my belief that if the team has a sensitive, that person should do a walk-through first before any contamination of the site from the rest of the team. However, the sensitive's activities could contaminate the physical evidence as well. All these scenarios are speculation. The main point is that you are systematic in what you do.

Bottom line, you should make a consistent and documented choice to help maintain credibility while continuing to improve your process. However, you choose to conduct the preliminary walk-through, the boundaries of the investigation should be set at that time.

Electromagnetic Frequency (EMF)

Contamination of the scene should be a primary concern to paranormal investigators. There is a parallel between a sterile environment and recognizing when there isn't one. EMF Field is a dirty subject in that many things emit fields, such as pipes or wiring; clean readings without eliminating the source means that any recording can potentially be contaminated. Make sure your search to document other fields is documented. EMF ghost stories that are debunked because you've found an emission source within an area with prior recorded activity can add to your credibility and can often be good stories in themselves.

Contemporary paranormal theory suggests that ghosts produce electromagnetic fields when they appear or are near, or they disrupt the fields that already exist. In either case you want to initially document if there are EMF disruptions in your initial walk-through.

Of the many universities that study the paranormal such as Princeton, Stanford, and the University of Arizona, one of the questions among the paranormal researchers is, is the detected magnetic field disruption measured by investigators a cause or an effect of the presence of ghosts? In other words, does a magnetic field open a doorway for the phenomena to pass through, or do the phenomena produce the magnetic resonance or fluctuation? To my knowledge, no one has captured a ghost to perform the se controlled tests to provide empirical evidence for either case. In my opinion, as an investigator, you have to respect both hypotheses and make a judgment call.

Influence of Electronics

If you enter the environment with multiple electronic gadgets, you can most certainly assume you are going to automatically disrupt the electromagnetic field. While in the Navy, I was an operations specialist. My job was to gather visual, auditory, and electronic data, decipher it, interpret it, and disseminate it to the proper channels. Visual information can be distorted due to optical abnormalities and atmospheric conditions. Audio frequencies can fluctuate due to sensor irregularities, speed, distance, and atmospherics. Electronic and magnetic frequencies can alter due to varying energy outputs and the presence of solidified metals. Trust that if you walk into an environment with your cell phone activated and GPS enabled, you are disrupting the very evidence you seek to identify. If you string electric cords throughout the environment, you will be actively causing electromagnetic disruptions. If you transmit using radios via walkie-talkies, you are disrupting the atmosphere with radio frequency energy. If you allow multiple people to meander the site prior to the investigation, you are unsettling the very fabric you wish to investigate.

The Association for the Scientific Study of Anomalous Phenomena (ASSAP) is a British paranormal education and research charity dedicated to explaining paranormal phenomena through scientific research. ASSAP also offers an Approved ASSAP Investigator's course (AAI). This organization can provide useful information to any paranormal investigation. In Maurice Townsend's article, "The Haunted Bed" (assap.uc.uk), he refers to the findings of Michael Persinger whose research determined that low-frequency magnetic fields can cause susceptible individuals to hallucinate. Because the standard EMF detector used by most ghost hunters cannot detect these frequencies, ASSAP member Dr. Jason Braithwaite designed the Magnetic Anomaly Detection System (MADS). Braithwaite refers to these low-frequency hallucinations as Experience-Induced Fields (EIF). A study of Muncaster Castle in Cumbria, United Kingdom, conducted by Braithwaite, resulted in supportive findings that there was evidence of an unexplained higher magnetic field variation over the haunted bed, which would correlate to the many haunted experiences reported by visitors and investigators of the castle. Braithwaite has been investigating Muncaster Castle for over a decade, and the case for this location being haunted is very strong and the monitoring of the events must be consistent and continuous. This is a truly comprehensive, paranormal investigation. Determining what is caused by human interaction and what is caused by the unexplained needs to be an investigator's priority.

Consider this: everywhere a person goes, they disturb the surroundings, alter physical evidence, and leave behind traces. Minimize these influences to maintain investigative credibility and ensure the events and evidence you collect are not something that is a result of your own doing.

Identifying External Influences

Ensure that you are aware of the location's surroundings and identify anything that could potentially affect the site. Things such as chemical plants, large metal objects, high voltage electricity, radio frequency energy, and unstable foundations can all lead to discrepancies in your instrumentation. I have seen ghost hunters become very excited when their magnetic compass acts strangely when in or near a large metal ship, or when their radios fail or act strangely when they are inside the ship, surrounded by metal. These are naturally occurring and explainable reactions and nothing out of the norm. This is why it is so necessary for a paranormal investigator to have experts they can call on, in many different fields. These professionals will be able to interpret the reaction of a given technology within the environment in which it malfunctioned.

The Use of a Medium

Whether or not you believe in their talents but have the privilege of a working relationship with one who shares your same objective, the use of a sensitive or clairvoyant can add a different perspective or approach to an investigation and its credibility. By drawing on additional attributes and skill sets, the lead investigator will be able to compile information for consideration. These supplementary additions may be the keys to opening additional avenues and provide the possibilities or information that fills in the gaps.

When deciding to work with a sensitive, confirm their credibility through competency, training, and longevity in their art. Their resume and philosophy should match and be able to add credibility to the group. No matter how active their role, they will be closely considered by those who evaluate your team's work.

Establishing Communication

Obviously, establishing communication with other worldly beings would be the ultimate goal for any paranormal investigator. So far, it appears the only consistently used human communication link between the dead and the living is through the interaction with a medium. Whether using divination instruments such as dowsing rods, pendulums, or Tarot cards, you are relying completely on the information provided by the sensitive. Participants need to trust in the person providing the interpretation.

There are certainly other forms of communication that can be attempted such as ghost, spirit, and echo boxes. While these electronics are experimental, that is the whole point, trying something different. However, I typically stick to what I understand in both audio and video. Most of what I find is either before or after the investigation. I have hundreds of hours of audio since 2015 that I have not reviewed for EVP. In my opinion, EVP often has some of the most consistent and interesting evidence of paranormal communication.

Use of passive voice. Based on current beliefs, mainly substantiated through Hollywood depictions of what spirits will or won't understand, most paranormalists would say the best way to communicate with the dead is through their native language. However, many mediums and spiritualists communicate through feelings and emotions, translating these to their spoken language. This is presumed when using instrumental trans-communication (ITC) methods such as radios, television, and other electronics the language will be understood by those on the receiving end.

However, because there are difficulties in viewing spirits or entities, one can only assume there would be audio difficulties as well. Each may experience the other's side in an altered time, either sped up or slowed down. They could be carried on an entirely different frequency or different plane. When choosing audible communication, one should use a very simple and brief message. Much like using a weak radio signal, the greeter should repeat the message in a strong, respectful voice, slowly and more than once. Playing 20 questions with the dead may not be the most productive way to establish communication.

In a case where you believe you know the spirit's name, you should use it to address them. While living, most people respond to their name favorably and we can assume it would be the same when deceased.

Use of Bait. This is a tactic often believed by ghost hunters to be a viable option when attempting to elicit a response from the dead. Having an item near and dear to the deceased is a reasonable instrument to entice communication when reaching for contact from the other side. Childhood dolls and toys, personal writings, clothing, hair locks and such seem to be possible lures.

Use of Aggression. The use of aggression toward any paranormal entity serves no purpose, and from what I have seen, results in no reaction at all. Stay away from bullying tactics.

However, if you feel the use of aggression toward a paranormal entity may be effective for locations like prisons where an aggressive history is expected and might be mirrored, follow your instincts. But keep in mind what that does to your emotional state. This is a good time for a few self-reflective questions. Are you putting out the kind of energy you want coming back to you? Are you opening yourself up for attack? Are you compromising the way you would morally behave to another being of the universe for entertainment?

My recommendation: Whatever you do, just don't be a jerk.

CHAPTER 24

Collecting Evidence

Forensic science is often referred to as forensics and generally means the scientific examination of evidence. In law enforcement there are two branches of forensic science: criminalistics and forensics. Criminalistics refers to technical applications to reveal evidentiary information, while forensics refers to the identity of the biological and physical condition through medical examination. Because many paranormal investigations are traumatic or criminal in nature, it would benefit all paranormal investigators to have an understanding of the uses and limitations of criminalistics techniques.

Criminalistics

There are many types of criminalist evaluations, and they are always evolving with the discovery of new methods and technologies. Here are some of the most used:

Wet Chemistry. Chemicals designed that when applied reveal the presence of another reactive substance. For example, a chemical spray called Luminol is designed to react with iron in the blood, revealing a reaction when blood is found. If an investigator suspects blood evidence was cleaned up, they can use Luminol to uncover the microscopic traces left behind.

Instrumental Chemistry. The process of using scientific instruments to investigate the properties of a material. Is it human or animal, of this Earth or extraterrestrial? There are many examples, such as using a microscope to identify hair or fibers, a laser to measure a materials reaction to heat, or handheld analyzers employed to test and categorize drugs in the field.

Firearms and Tool-Marks. Chemical tests and microscopic analysis of firearm components and tools to determine whether they have or have not been used in an event. The Modified Griess Test is an example of a test used by firearms examiners to determine a muzzle-to-garment distance. The test detects the nitrite by-product residue of the combustion of smokeless gunpowder. Also, microscopic striations can be measured using specialized cameras to determine unique patterns left behind by a tool used for prying or striking.

Questioned Documents. Methods of analysis to determine the validity of a document, usually applied only if it is thought the document could be a forgery. The study would concentrate on types of patterns unique to the writer like blunt starts and stops, pen lifts and hesitations, tremors, corrective marks, and speed and pressure. This analysis is also applied to confirm or discredit official, noteworthy, or valuable documents, for instance wills, original works, and records.

Latent Prints. Marks left on an object that require a process to be revealed. Examiners can use an alternate light source (ALS) or lasers, apply vaporized cyanoacrylate (superglue), or fingerprint powders in order to reveal what the naked eye cannot see.

Photography. Capturing an image using conventional or unconventional means. Like any other skill, photographers should spend time studying their equipment, understanding the influences of light sources, and being aware of the difficulties in capturing objects in motion.

Lie Detection. Physiological evaluations to determine whether an individual's body reacts in a stressful manner, common with someone who is lying. There are many different machines designed to provide indicators of deception. Traditional lie detection is rarely needed in a paranormal investigation.

Forensics. Forensics is the most complicated of the technical services used in law enforcement investigations. Medical certifications and licenses are required to perform most forensic examinations intended to be used for official law proceedings.

Pathology: The study of disease.

Serology: The study of blood.

Toxicology: The study of toxins.

Odontology: The study of the structure and diseases of the teeth.

Psychiatry: The study of normal and abnormal behavior.

Paranormal investigations use the above same two avenues of forensic science, forensics and criminalistics. On most cases, ghost hunters use instrumentation to capture visual, audio, electronic and other phenomena much like criminalists do. They also psychologically assess witnesses' behavior to determine the validity of their experience or legitimacy of their story and pay attention to signs and symptoms of mental disease.

However, for paranormal research, I would not limit this to traditional forensic science. I believe the paranormal detective should incorporate genetics, genealogy, and anomalistics to the forensic side. Anomalistics is defined as the use of scientific methods to study phenomena that fall outside current understanding. This would include ufology, cryptozoology, and parapsychology. I would also add a third and separate category which I refer to as *paralistics*. Paralistics are what I identify as specifically designed methods and technical instruments used for investigating and locating paranormal phenomena as it pertains to ghost hunting. Cryptozoology and ufology typically rely on current detection technologies and practices, and there does not appear to be anything truly reliable outside these ordinary methods.

It is obvious that some of the forensic medicine disciplines are not needed in most paranormal investigations; however, a few could be considered in specialized situations. Let's say a person has requested you to conduct a residential investigation for a haunting. And let's say you happen upon an old trunk containing clothes and personal effects—the Holy Grail! Upon close examination, you may be able to recover a human hair or other material germane to the investigation. Should someone decide to pay for the test, a DNA genetics analysis can be ordered through a private lab and the identity of the hair could be established, especially if you can identify to whom the trunk belonged or have any relative who would be willing to provide a buccal (cheek) swab as comparison. DNA coding through private industry can cost about $120 per test. These tests would not stand up in court; however, they are legitimate for our purposes. DNA has become very inexpensive and is a great tool for answering many questions of heredity.

Paralistics

A specialized breakdown of these paralistic categories as used in paranormal investigations would be as follows:

Electromagnetic Field (EMF) Detector/Sensor. A detector that locates the electromagnetic field produced by a charged object. These detectors can pick up electromagnetic fields generated in and around anything that has an electrical charge, whether it is AC or DC. Often used by ghost hunters to detect fluctuations in electromagnetic fields. It is not a ghost detector.

Motion Detector. Most motion sensors are referred to as passive infrared sensors, specifically calibrated to human body temperature. They are designed to go off when they detect rapidly changing thermal distortions. Some can detect movement through optical measurements.

Electronic Voice Phenomena (EVP) Detection. Most EVPs are recorded onto an analog or digital recording device. To effectively capture EVPs, one should use both analog and digital formats in conjunction with one another. The audio captured is typically rated as follows:

Class A: Easily understood by almost anyone with little or no dispute.
Class B: Usually characterized by warping of the voice in certain syllables.
Class C: Characterized by excessive warping. Class C are the lowest in volume, often nothing more than whispers and are the hardest to understand.

Infrared Thermometer. An infrared thermometer measures thermal radiation and allows users to measure temperature in applications where conventional sensors cannot be employed. Specifically, in cases dealing with moving objects, or where non-contact measurements are required because of contamination or hazardous reasons or where distances are too great. It is not a ghost detector.

Carbon Monoxide Detectors. Used for safety in dangerous locations and as a possible detection device of paranormal activity.

Infrasound Monitors. These monitors are typically run by geological survey consulting companies or by many different governments. Their information can often be accessed on the Internet.

Dowsing Rods and Divining Instruments. According to controlled tests, there is no scientific basis regarding the use of dowsing rods or other divining instruments, other than random chance. However, paranormal investigations may have uses for these devices.

Paranormalist theory is that the instruments, in conjunction with human emotion or intuition, can assist the diviner in answering questions or locating areas of interest.

Geiger Counter. This device detects radiation such as alpha particles, beta particles and gamma rays and is useful in locating either higher than normal radiation levels such as indicative of UFO activity or determining if your vintage orange Fiesta dinnerware contains radioactive uranium oxide. The Geiger counter is a delicate tool that is difficult to use because it requires a long-life radiation source to measure its calibrations. It can easily be misread or misunderstood if the user is not practiced in radiation principles.

Magnetic Compass. This type of compass consists of a small, lightweight magnet balanced on a nearly frictionless pivot point whose needle (arrow) nearly always points to magnetic north. Many people think this indicates the North Pole, but it is pointing toward a large iron ore deposit in Canada. This is why, depending on where you stand on the Earth, your compass will require a declination adjustment for proper navigation.

Ghost Box. An electronic device that some ghost hunters claim helps in communication with the dead. It is my belief that you should not use this as anything more than an electronic Magic 8-Ball. I purchased a ghost box online and it was nothing more than a digital radio with its scan stop disabled. It scanned through channels picking up a random word here and there. Fun, but worthless for real investigations. Unless you believe your ghost transmits on 98.1 FM. Maybe the spirit was an old DJ, who knows?

Para-Forensics

Para-Forensics involved nontraditional approaches that, at face value, do not initially appear to be related or have evidentiary value. Para-forensics are additional, often academic, avenues to explore and establish a clearer picture of the causes of the reported occurrence.

Anomalistics. The use of scientific methods to study phenomena that falls outside current understanding.

Psychology. The scientific study of the human mind and how its functions affect perception and behavior.

Parapsychology. The study of mental phenomena that are excluded from or inexplicable by orthodox scientific psychology, i.e., hypnosis, telepathy, clairvoyance, psychokinesis, etc.

Genealogy. The study and tracing of the lines of descent or development in an organism. Specifically, in this case, humans.

Genetics. The study of heredity and the genetic properties or features. In this case, humans.

Use of Technology

The use of technology is a hotly debated topic in the world of ghost hunting. There are several theories about the exclusive use of technology, the exclusive use of human interaction, and the combination of the two. It is a conversation all paranormal groups should have. Whatever you decide, stick with it for a defined period of time. Once you feel you have exhausted its expectations, then switch to another technology, and stick with it for a defined amount of time. This will allow for a truer evaluation of the tactics used.

For example, say you have a case where a person was murdered at 10 PM, November 1, 1882, inside a specific residence considered to be haunted. If you have the opportunity to access this location over a prolonged period of time, try this experiment. Do an initial visit with no technology. If you are lucky to be joined by a medium or other sensitive, use the time in an attempt to observe events using only the senses. Now, some reading this are aghast that I would pass up the opportunity to capture an apparition on video, an EVP on audio, a spike in EMF, or a fluctuation in temperature.

My answer to you is to practice focusing and honing your own internal technology and experience the environment first before you bring in the science.

Most technology emits its own frequencies, EMFs, and disruptions. What if this electronic seep disrupts the source of the phenomena to begin with? What if, for whatever reason, the technology is the thing that is preventing the event from happening in the first place? It would make sense that you would penetrate the area with the least amount of residual influence as possible, unless you believe it is the technology that triggers the occurrence. What if it is only the human experience that can sense and define such occurrences? After all, isn't that where all this began? Long ago, before the spirit box? Before the EMF detector? Wasn't it just the person?

So, I suggest that investigators take incremental steps to their approach and spend the time practicing with technology. I ask again, what if these events are purely human? Do not minimize the contribution of someone who feels they are tuned in to these things. Setting up experiments is great, but don't spend your entire time staring down at your instruments.

Collection and Storage

I have spoken with many ghost hunters who report great recordings or photos only to later lose them due to a technology malfunction. To ensure this doesn't happen to you, always back up your computer photo and audio files, and save them to a USB flash drive, or to the Cloud. At the very least, attach the files and email them to yourself. This is a cheap and effective way to save them. These actions will help ensure loss is minimized. However, whenever you truly have what you believe to be paranormal evidence, burn this data to a DVD. This will be the best guard against any technology malfunctions and will provide an actual physical record.

Each case you work on will consist of (1) written documentation, (2) computer files of photos, videos, audios, and data research, and (3) physical evidence. Whenever starting a project, create a physical file to store all records collected. This can be a three-ring binder with your printed documentation, clear sleeve inserts for DVDs and flash drives, and a clear sealable pouch for other various document- and evidence-related material.

When you die, the experiences you had in life will die with you unless you document them. Strive to create a chain of documentation and evidence that speaks for itself. A product that anyone can pick up, see and understand what you produced. Let your documentation and evidence speak for itself.

CHAPTER 25

Documentation

If it's not documented, it didn't happen. That is the standard rule for law enforcement actions. In your report, if you neglected to dictate that the Miranda Rights were read to the suspect, it didn't happen. If you did not articulate why you established probable cause to arrest the person, you didn't have it. Within the court of law, documentation is everything; the people expect it. That is why it is so important that paranormal investigators document their investigations; the people expect it.

Three Common Types of Documentation

There are many ways paranormal investigators can document their actions. Whatever method you choose, remain consistent with it and attempt to refine it to better your skills and the final product.

Written Reports. The least impressive (and easiest to review and analyze) is a written report. Always transcribe a written report in a computer format to allow ease of readability and research. You might consider transcribing notes soon after the investigation to have the events fresh in your mind and maintain the ability to clarify initial points.

This is why when criminals and politicians have to provide their email histories; they print them out. They know it will take months for examiners to go over the hard copies. If they copied and pasted using a computer, reviewers could more easily search for key words relevant to the inquiry using digital search methods. Electronic copies are best. They are effortlessly shared and easily researched.

Video Documentation. Video is possibly the most effective type of documentation because it is not a written recreation. You can see and hear the original actions and statements of all involved and corroborate with witness testimony or prior reports. While people like and trust video more than the written word, in some cases the audio is not understandable, and the picture could be missing what is important. These discrepancies have to be resolved and addressed. In some cases, you may want to consult with a professional in the video business.

Reviewing video and looking for specific items during hours and hours of recordings is a difficult and timely task. If you are going to rely on video as your documentation, ensure you keep all the original videos, make a copy, and then take the time to edit the duplicate footage down to a manageable length which would contain the pertinent information and events. At bare minimum, edit out all the dead time and leave at least 15 seconds before and after the targeted event.

Audio Recordings. Audio recordings have advantages over reports but are not as convincing as video. Like video, audio also has challenges. In certain cases, the sound is garbled and open to misinterpretation. This is where much of the EVP (Electronic Voice Phenomena) debate comes from.

There are several prominent recordings in the public that are very controversial and open to mass interpretation. Radio personality, researcher, and audio professional Dave Schrader, host of *Midnight in the Desert,* has firsthand experience with such a debate. On his former show *Darkness Radio,* Dave had a guest claiming connections to the Rhine Institute who shared what he felt was the holy grail of his research, a very mysterious EVP in what sounded like a foreign language. This man said it was one of the best EVPs ever captured, and he worked extensively to identify the language. He was even joined by others, including audio professionals. Even linguists could not identify the language, or what it meant: "aay vee ess aud ee oah deh moe." Only after the man played it backward did he hear his interpretation of the message: "It's my baby, save it." This is the message he shared with the world as proof of the paranormal.

However, after being reviewed by Dave Schrader and his staff, the reported EVP was identified as a common audio watermark originating from AVS Audio, a software company. This watermark was imbedded randomly in their free demo products to encourage users to purchase the full versions: "aay vee ess aud ee oah deh moe." Anyone, even seasoned detectives, can make mistakes like these. The key is to recognize those mistakes and move on.

Be careful and open-minded about the evidence you collect. Listen to others' interpretations and ask yourself, what is the most likely explanation? Getting so invested in trying to prove the paranormal can discredit your methods.

Reviewing audio and searching for specific items in hours and hours of digital or analog recording can be a tedious process. If you are going to rely solely on audio as your documentation, ensure that you keep all the original soundtracks and take the time to edit a copy of the recordings down to a manageable length containing pertinent information and events. Like video, edit out all the dead time and leave at least 15 seconds before and after the targeted event.

Whatever method you choose, strive for quality and clarity because there will be people reading, watching and listening. The product you put forward will oftentimes be your only representative; you will be judged by it.

CHAPTER 26

Providing Closure

It is always interesting to hear someone reference the end of a violent or particularly tragic criminal case by commenting on how the end will now provide the family with "closure." I agree. When a person is missing for years, most people would want to know whether or not that person is dead, and even if they have passed, it does provide some sort of closure. When a murder or rapist goes to court and is found guilty, that provides a form of closure. However, victims will tell you there is never really an end, merely a transition to another form of grief. My 93-year-old mother still cries when she tells the story of how her younger twin siblings died on a cold and rainy night in a drafty farmhouse in rural Kentucky. She describes how they were left bare and open in the cold and dark downstairs breezeway to slow their decomposition. How she had to walk past them several times that night going to and from the kitchen and her ailing mother's bedroom. Each time, wanting to cover them up to keep them warm.

That was 1933.

Lost in Time

There are many times in life when there is no closure—this includes formal investigations. Sometimes, there are no leads to follow, and the event remains just what it was—an event. In some incidents there are multiple witnesses, trace evidence, and background occurrences, yet there is no determination of what caused it. Property crimes detectives know this very well; the item was there and now it's gone. Sometimes, that's just the way it is. Something happened without explanation. Millions of human events and tragedies have occurred and gone unnoticed by others; they simply disappear into the hole in the sky—nothing witnessed, and nothing remembered. The tragedy never to be known, the pain never realized.

In any case, there comes a point when must make a judgment. Sometimes, in criminality, that judgment is filing charges against a person. Sometimes, it is knowing a person committed the offense but without enough probable cause to file for the arrest. And sometimes, you simply don't know. In the cases of paranormal events, you have the same dilemmas. At some point, must make a determination: you have to decide whether the paranormal event is factual or not. This can be decided only if there is enough information to make the decision. If not, you may have to suspend the search until additional leads surface, or simply close the case as unfounded with no phenomenon evidence or natural explanation supporting the occurrence.

Endings

So, there you are. You've got the ghost story, conducted your research, interviewed your witnesses, investigated the site, and reviewed your collected data and information. Eventually, after a total review of the evidence and circumstances of the phenomena, someone has to come to a conclusion. That conclusion is typically based on an interpretation of the facts of the case and sits in your hands. How convinced are you? Are you willing to stake your reputation on your decision, or do you need more information? Maybe you need more time? In some cases, the team leader assigns the closure to the investigation, other times it is a team consensus or vote. Whatever you decide, there is a time when you will have to conclude the case, set it aside, and move on; that is your job. And often it is not that simple. If your client truly believes in skyfish, the fact that you discover they are actually flying insects captured on a low-resolution camera will not change their mind.

Richard P. Feynman found this out when he was selected to be a part of the space shuttle Challenger's explosion investigation. The brittleness of the joint seal was the hypothesis, and that is what Feynman wanted to concentrate on. He was right. However, in some investigations, it is not about making a ruling quickly and efficiently. Sometimes there are other considerations to be made. Other emotions and sensitivities to be considered. Cultural implications. Politics. Friendships. All these things can affect the decision-making process. In stretching yourself past ghost hunting, broadening yourself beyond paranormal investigating, and immersing yourself in the art of paranormal detecting, you will be much better equipped to make this ruling.

When dealing with the paranormal, decide when things need to slow down so that the inevitable can be digested and further considered by those who doubt you. Steady yourself against quick conclusions; there is often more to the story and the evidence.

Conclusion

Remember, no matter what happens, your investigative job is to gather facts, determine truths, evaluate evidence, and provide a verdict. Sometimes, because of the unknowns, you may not be able to make an informed decision. And that's okay as well. Sometimes there is no answer, simply more questions. The real point is to continue asking the questions and striving for a conclusion.

I hope the fact-finding and organizational concepts I have discussed in this book will help broaden your perspective and open new conversations with your colleagues. The goal of this quest is to always learn and grow. I have no doubt, one day someone is going to figure this all out.

I wish you the best of luck in your adventures in the dark, and your transition from ghost hunter to paranormal detective.

Appendix
Investigation Review List

The following should be considered when conducting a paranormal investigation of a site that is alleged to have paranormal activity:

1. Document the legend as the story is told.
2. Interview witnesses to phenomena.
3. Compile historical research noting dates and times of sightings.
4. Identify area experts and obtain their statements and opinions.
5. Summarize the historical event and contrast it with the story.
6. Survey and map the location.
7. Conduct a walk-through and sketch the area identifying hazards.
8. Conduct a threat assessment and identify any dangers.
9. Create an investigative operations plan and assign tasks.
10. Brief team members via email, etc.
11. Inventory and gather equipment.
12. Conduct an onsite operational briefing.
13. Conduct a daylight walk-through.
14. Conduct brief-backs with members explaining their assignments.
15. Initial nighttime walk-through of the psychic/medium (if desired).
16. Initial nighttime walk-through with no electronics.
17. Deployment of the electronics.
18. Monitoring of the electronics without outside influences.
19. Slowly introduce investigators with full electronics.
20. Stationary observation of the investigator and equipment.

21. Investigators interactive / experimentation time.
22. Equipment recovery.
23. Investigator's final sweep-through.
24. Secure the site.
25. Conduct a team de.briefing.
26. Analyze the gathered data.
27. Interpret the data.
28. Compile a chronological and concise report of the events.
29. Articulate a conclusion.

Bibliography

Belanger, J. (2011). *The World's Most Haunted Places,* Revised Edition. Pompton Plains, NJ: New Page Books.

Bennett, W. W., & Hess, K. (2004). *Management and Supervision in Law Enforcement,* 4th edition. Belmont, CA: Thomson Wadsworth.

Broome, F. (2007). *The Ghosts of Austin: Who They Are and Where to Find Them.* Lancaster, PA: Schiffer Publishing.

Brown, A. (2012). *The Big Book of Texas Ghost Stories.* Mechanicsburg, PA: Stackpole Books.

Carey, T., & Schmitt, D. (2007). *Witness to Roswell: Unmasking the 60-Year Cover-up.* Franklin Lakes, NJ: New Page Books.

Dobrin, A. (2013). "Your memory isn't what you think it is." *Psychology Today,* post July 16, 2013.

Dolan, R. (2000). *UFOs and the National Security State: An unclassified history, Volume One: 1941-1973.* Rochester, NY: Keyhole Publishing Company.

Feynman, R. P. (1988). *What Do You Care What Other People Think?: Further adventures of a curious character.* New York, NY: Bantam Books.

Glenday, C. (1999). *The UFO Investigator's Handbook. The practical guide to researching, identifying, and documenting unexplained sightings.* Philadelphia, PA. Running Press Book Publishers.

Guiley, R. E. (2013). *The Djinn Connection. The Hidden Links Between Djinn, Shadow People, ETs, Nephilim, Archons, Reptilians and Other Entities.* New Milford, CT: Visionary Living Inc.

Haydon, S. E. (1897, April 17). "A windmill demolishes it." *The Dallas Morning News.*

Montefiore, S. S. (2008). *Histories Monsters: 101 Villains from Vald the Impaler to Adolf Hitler.* New York, NY: Metro Books.

Schiller D, Delgado MR. "Overlapping neural systems mediating extinction, reversal and regulation of fear." *Trends in Cognitive Sciences* 2010; 14: 268-276.

Skurnick, L., (Eds.). (1997). *Mysteries of the Unknown. United States of America.* Time Life Books.

About the Author

Greg Lawson, M.Ed., has traveled to over 40 countries visiting some of Earth's strangest sites and conducting his own investigation of their paranormal histories. Greg is a 26-year law enforcement officer, professional investigator, police academy instructor, college educator, and former expert witness for investigative procedures. He researches and investigates human paranormal experience and locations known for spiritual or unusual activity. He has authored two books on the subject and specializes in providing alternative perspectives to explain human experience.

Greg is a 10-year military veteran with the U.S. Army, Navy, and Air Force, and is a lake patrol and underwater recovery team sergeant in Central Texas. He uses the thousands of hours of training he has received through his profession and his experience as a detective along with his master's degree in Education to study paranormal human experience and physical anomalies.

With deployments to Central America, Europe, Northern Africa, Asia, the Middle East, and two Western Pacific sea deployments, Greg is a lifetime member of the Veterans of Foreign Wars (VFW) and holds an honorary Admiral commission in the Texas Navy.

Greg received his bachelor's degree in applies arts and sciences and his master's degree in education, specializing in complex adaptive human systems. He is an alumnus of Texas State University.

CPSIA information can be obtained
at www.ICGtesting.com
Printed in the USA
LVHW111310120819
627332LV00001BA/102/P

9 781942 157489